Mastering
the
Rich Mindset

Mastering
the
Rich Mindset

Ravi Kant Kashyap
More than 40years' in the field of
FINANCIAL PLANNING

60 Financial Tips Which took me 9 years to learn,
But you can learn in 9 minutes....

Compossed by
Vidyapati Sharma
Mob - 9871911248
E-mail-vpatisharma@gmail.com

You can't change the mind
of another living soul
You can only plant an
Idea and hope that
They allow it to grow
-Erin Chatters-

Introduction

The rich mindset is a powerful way of thinking that enables individuals to achieve financial success and abundance. This is all about mastering the rich mindset and how it can transform your life.

To develop a wealthy mindset, you must learn to think and act like a wealthy person. This means developing a positive attitude towards money, investing wisely, and taking calculated risks.

We will bring together all the principles and strategies of the rich mindset and show you how to put them into practice in your own life. We will provide a step-by-step guide to developing a rich mindset and achieving financial success and abundance.

We will explore how to set and achieve financial goals using the principles of the rich mindset in this book, like.....

Developing a Wealthy Mindset

Setting and Achieving Financial Goals

Building Wealth Through Entrepreneurship

Investing for Financial Freedom

Overcoming Obstacles to Financial Success

Thanks to

Ashutosh Kashyap (my son)

Who inspired me to write this Book.

ACKNOWLEDGEMENTS

I am grateful to Mr. Kulbir Singh Chawla &
Mrs. Usha Singh Kashyap (my wife) for editing
this book.

Also thankful to Mr. Shailender Saxena &
Mr. Debasis Chattopadhyay for guidance &
suggestions

DREAMS DON'T WORK UNLESS YOU DO

In the whole world, Dreams or even people have died due to their self-doubts and for not taking action to translate their dreams into action. Because of Self-doubt and Mindset, the thoughts never become reality.

It is our habit to find an easy way to succeed without knowing that it is not the permanent solution. Those who can't change their minds can't change anything.

Due to not taking action in time, the work cannot be done and even ample opportunities can be missed.

Keep on tracking your mind in the right direction.
Be the Master of Your Mind.

Usha Singh Kashyap

Contents

Why This Book?

This financial knowledge that I am sharing with you, was ever given to me when I was doing my job then by now I may have been one of the billionaires.

For the last 40 years, I am doing Financial &Tax Planning and guiding my clients on how to save Tax, but I never tried to find out how they are earning and increasing their wealth day by day. In our school and college, we are taught about different subjects but none of the professors teach us how to earn money or how to become financially secure.

I discovered that to whom so ever I guided had started a business and a few were millionaires, but I was doing my job and was working hard to earn my monthly payout. As I came to understand the game of making money, I quit my full-time job and started doing consultancy. I realised that the income should not be only from one source. The main income should be from our salary and the other source of income are for payment of our bills (expenses)

This book contains all my experience and the knowledge that I gained from my learning and through my personal experience which I want to share.

I decided to give a few tips for making money to the younger generation so that they may get the freedom to enjoy rich life through financial knowledge which they do not get from their institutions.

If you are one of those who believe that hard work and honesty, alone, will bring riches. It is not so. Formal education will give you a living whereas self-education will make you a fortune. There are so many questions in your mind such as:

1. Is there any shortcut method to becoming rich?
2. Is doing only a job can make you rich?
3. How to earn money?
4. Why did the Rich get Richer?
5. How can you be careful while taking a loan?
6. How do the Rich minimize their Tax burden?
7. How the income can be compounded?
8. What is the mindset of Rich People?
9. What the Rich People teach their Kids?
10. What are the income-earning options?
11. Which are safe investments?

I have tried to give answers to all the questions so that you can easily understand the three main aspects of money

1.How to Earn

2.How to Save

3.How to Invest

I survive because the fire inside me burns brighter than the fire around me.

Ravi Kant Kashyap

The Inspiration and Reason for this Book

This book is helpful for those who want to enjoy life with the freedom of finance and learn to invest wisely.

Having money is a form of power. But what is more powerful is financial education. Money comes and goes, but if you have an education about how money works, you gain control over it and can build wealth.

Making Money or Getting Rich is a game that is played with knowledge, Strategy, Foresight, Patience, and Discipline

This book is a guide to the younger generation of 20 late 40 years of age. If you are not serious about your savings and have no pension on your retirement, then become serious.

Tomorrow is happening today. If you can't see it, if you don't know what's in the coming, you are going to be left behind. You must be willing to work hard and catch up with the changing times. And things are moving so fast you may never catch up—ever.

Painful impact of Covid-19

The pandemic period has seen salaries slashed, increments held, and variable pays put on hold. The household budgets of millions of families have gone haywire. The situation is worse for those who have lost their jobs. How do you keep your finance on track?

Lesson from Covid 19

1. Life is short

2. Jobs are Temporary

3. Health is Wealth

4. Always save money

5. We need God to survive

Effective utilization of Quarantine period:

Acquiring, NEW SKILLS, MORE KNOWLEDGE as you never lacked time, you may lack discipline.

"The best way to deal with an impending job crisis is to prepare for the worst and plan your finances accordingly."

Find ways to increase your income. Reskill, upgrade and fine-tune your existing abilities, start freelancing, and monetize your passions.

THE GAME OF MONEY IS TO LEARN

How to Earn………………….(Earn Money)…….Stage-1

How to Save………………......(Save Money)….......Stage-2

How to Invest………………..(Invest Money)….......Stage-3

How to Create Wealth….…….(Multiply Money)......Stage-4

How to be Consistent……...(Maintain Money).....Stage-5

Look, Listen & Learn

And most important: Health is wealth

Game of money is a balance of, what to save, what to invest

Money is Earned in three ways:

1. Power

2. Intellect and Wisdom

3. Knowledge

Money and Wealth represent: Goddess Lakshmi

Intellect and Wisdom represent: Lord Ganesha

Knowledge represents: Goddess Saraswati

These three gods are worshipped together **to invite abundance alongside insight.**

They embody knowledge, wealth, and power.

Hence, Lakshmi is always worshipped along with Ganesha on Diwali. Gaining wealth without intellect will only result in misusing the wealth. So, one must first acquire the intelligence to spend the wealth in the right manner. Therefore, Lakshmi and Ganesha are worshipped together.

On Diwali, we celebrate and worship wealth. But true wealth comes only when a person has knowledge or talent. It's said Lakshmi finds the home of the learned only. Since Saraswati is the goddess of books and music (talent), even she is worshiped by Ganesha.

True wealth comes only when a person has knowledge or talent. And Goddess Lakshmi finds the home of the learned only.

Stage-1
Earn Money

How to Earn?

Earned income is the primary source of income and it is the root of all wealth, it includes wages, salaries, profit from the business, and also earnings from self-employment. There are three types of income.

1. Earned Income (Active Income)

2. Investment Income

3. Passive Income

Earned Income

This is a primary income that is earned by our actions, it includes income earned from salary. The growth of salary happens at a fixed rate. If a person wants to increase his salary, he has to work more hours. And moreover, salaried income is one of the most highly taxed sources of income.

Investment Income

This income has no relation to the number of hours worked. It keeps on accruing over a period of time and is generated by selling investments that were made earlier.

Passive Income

It is another important source of income. This can be earned from rent, interest, or dividends. A person who is earning 25% of their income from passive sources is better off than a person who is earning 100% of their income in the form of a salary.

Passive Income is of two types

Digital Income

Non-Digital Income

The sources of Digital Income are:

1. Youtubing. To start your channel on the Youtube platform.

2. Blogging

3. Affiliate Marketing

4. E-Commerce

5. Online tutorial courses

6. Online Footage (Sell Stock Footage)

The sources of Non-Digital Income are:

1. Insurance Policies (Commission Income)

2. Real Estate (Rental Income)

3. Car Renting (Uber & Ola)

4. Books (E-book Income)

5. Mutual Fund / Stock Market

6. Airbnb (Accommodation Provider, owns no real estate.)

Passive Income can be earned through three angles:

1. Interest: Where do you have an interest

2. Investment: Where you can invest

3. Income: Where you can generate

Every working person should have some knowledge about how the different types of income can be used to generate wealth. However, it is surprising that many people do not focus on generating the second and third sources of income and hence are not able to make optimum utilization of their earning potential.

IF YOU DON'T WORK ON MAKING YOURSELF RICH YOU WILL HELP SOMEONE ELSE

Chapter One
Vision and Determination

It is not about overnight success or getting rich without any effort

"Change is the law of life. And those who look only to the past or the present are certain to miss the future." (John F. Kennedy)

There is no shortcut to wealth creation

If you need Daily Money   Do Labour

If you need Monthly Money   Do Job

If you need Lifetime Money   Do Business

College degrees are not needed to make a lot of money. Skills are required to earn.

Going to college, getting a good job, and providing a secure future for yourself and your family is all that it used to be, sure they teach you a lot in college. But none of the professors teaches you how to become financially secure.

In the last 25 years, globalization has led to 30% of job losses because of automation and advanced technology. Today one high-tech software system can do the work of many workers —and by automation will do it better, faster, and cheaper. Today, it's nearly impossible to get a "live" person on the phone when you call your credit card company—mortgage company—bank—

or insurance company. A machine that never makes mistakes—never takes a vacation—doesn't go on strike for higher wages—doesn't require a benefits package with a pension, answer your queries.

Tomorrow is happening today. If you can't see it, if you don't know what's coming, you are going to be left behind. You must be willing to work hard and catch up with the changing times. And things are moving so fast you may never catch up—ever.

We have made a habit of settling for less—setting for less as a lifestyle. This is the view of each and everyone out of us.

But everyone wants to be rich and wants to know a shortcut method to earn tons of money in a single shot. **You wouldn't plant a seed and then dig it up every few minutes to see if it has grown. Have patience, stop overthinking, and keep watering your seeds.** Fruits on a tree never grow in a day one has to care for and wait for a required period of time.

Prosperity needs time and patience. Money deposited in a term deposit can't be doubled within a fortnight. It requires a period of time maybe 10 years to double. Whereas on the basis of your financial knowledge and proper utilization of your investments the period from 10 years can be reduced to 5-6 years. This cannot be possible without proper planning & knowledge of money-earning.

A job is a really short-term solution to a long-term- problem. Those in jobs never think as their wages increase, taxes also increase and so do the other expenses in proportion to their salary increase.

LESSON: LEARN HOW TO EARN MONEY PASSIVELY

Chapter Two
Thought Clarity

Every decision in our lives requires clarity of thought.

And it's truly said: He who wishes to be rich in a day will be hanged in a year- (Leonardo da Vinci) & "There are no shortcuts to any place worth going." Beverly Sills)

Let me make you understand through a real case study of my assistant:

I was working as an Accounts Officer in a company. One of my account- assistants was from a lower middle class. He was living with his two younger brothers and one younger sister. From his small salary, he had to pay rent and school fees for his two brothers. I was surprised at how he was managing his family-expenses but he never tried to discuss his financial problems. He was active and punctual in his day-to-day work. He was always interested in learning something new from me so that he might improve his skill and could increase his income through part-time work.

He got married and his expenses increased. Now he used to travel on foot to save on his expenses. After a year he was blessed with a son and his expenses increased. He had to send his brothers and sisters away to his parents and their education was disturbed. He left the service and joined another company doing a job for more than 12 hours to earn more. But could not pursue it long and left that job. He took a shop on rent to start a business selling ladies' garments. Now he had fixed expenses to pay like rent for the shop and also had to arrange funds to invest in stocks to earn more. It was not easy for him to manage the shop as well. Since he had no salary income, he often had to take loans from friends and many times failing commitment to return on time. He had to use his credit cards for the purchase of stocks. But the credit was increasing with every passing day, and he would not be in a position to pay even the interest on the loan. Finally, he chose to shut his shop, again searching for a job one day he came to me for help. He said he was so tired by now that he was not in a position to make the correct decisions.

Everyone wants to be rich without proper planning which is never possible.

LESSON: DON'T USE CREDIT IF YOU DON'T HAVE CASH

Chapter Three
Basics and Fundamentals

To start with how to PLANT SEEDS OF MONEY

Money is a symbol of the economic health of the nation. When money is circulating freely in your life, you are economically healthy. Do not ever regard money as evil or filthy. If you do, you cause it to take wings and fly away from you. **Remember that you lose what you condemn. You cannot attract what you criticize.**

RULES OF MONEY: DON'T BE A HATER OF MONEY

Having money is a form of power. But what is more powerful is financial education. Money comes and goes, but if you have an education about how money works, you gain control over it and build wealth.

If you want to be rich, you have to learn to earn money. The best thing about money is that it works 24 hours a day and can work for generations. But our school focuses only on teaching us to work for money, not how to get money's power. If you want to be rich, you need to be financially literate and know how to read financial statements.

RULES OF MONEY: IT'S A GAME, LEARN HOW IT WORKS

Before proceeding with "Plantation seeds of money", first we have to understand the basic principles of financial management.

The basic purpose to learn about financial management is to present a complete financial picture of the business with the help of two financial statements

a. Profit & Loss Account: shows the total Revenues & Expenses incurred during the accounting period. Excess of Revenues over Expenses is the Net Profit or Net Income. If total Expenses are in Excess of Revenues, the Net Result is a Loss.

b. Balance Sheet: The Balance Sheet is prepared to ascertain the true financial position of a business. It displays the properties, Assets owned by the business on the right-hand side, Liabilities to outsiders, and amounts Invested by owners as Capital on the left-hand side.

1 Assets: Anything which will enable the firm to get cash or a benefit in the future such as Land, Building, Stock, Bonds, Mutual funds, Cash and Bank balances.

2. Liabilities: It is the amount owing to the creditors for goods or services received or for money borrowed such as Creditors, Bills payable, Bank overdraft, long-term loans

Assets and Liability

As explained by Robert T. Kiyosaki in his book "Rich Dad Poor Dad"

An asset is something that puts money in your pocket whether you work or not. A liability is something that takes money out of your pocket.

Rich people acquire assets. The poor and middle class acquire liabilities (purchase of house/asset on loan) and they think of them as their assets.

Chapter Four
Ways to Improve Financial Health

Knowledge is the Vehicle that will change your life

Learn how to read the Cash Flow Statement

With the help of a cash flow statement, one can understand whether he is a rich, poor, or middle-class person.

Cash Flow Statement

Cash flow is a financial statement that shows how much cash is saved or left in hand after making all the expenses. Or one can say, a "**Cash Flow Statement**" reports the cash generated and used during a given period of time.

Positive **Cash Flow** indicates that a person's liquid assets are increasing, enabling it to settle debts, reinvest in its business, pay expenses, and provide a buffer against future financial challenges.

1.Cash Flow of a Poor Person:

Income (Salary) = Expenses (Taxes, Rent, Food, Transportation, clothes, education fee)

Income PA Rs. 5,00,000 -5,20,000 Expenses = Loan Rs.20,000

2.Cash Flow of a Middle-Class Person:

Income (Salary) = Expenses (Taxes, Car payments, credit card payments, education fee) **Liabilities** (Mortgage, car loans, credit card purchases, loans)

Income PA Rs. 10,00,000 -9,90,0000 Expenses = Saving Rs.10,000

3.Cash flow of a Rich Person: Income (Rental income, Dividend, Interest, Royalties) = **Expenses** (Taxes, mortgage payment) Assets (Real Estate, stocks, bonds, Intellectual property)

Income PA Rs. 50,00,000 -15,00,000 Expenses – 30,00,000 Investment= Saving Rs.5,00,000

An Investment of Rs. 30 lacs was used for the purchase of Assets (Real Estate, stocks, bonds, Intellectual property)

FORMULA FOR MAKING MONEY

"Keep expenses low, Reduce liabilities, Purchase income-generating assets"

Think of it this way: Once Money changes into your Asset, it becomes your employee. The best thing about money is that it works 24 hours a day to earn for you and can work for generations.

Anybody can wish for riches, and most people do, but only a few know that **a definite plan, plus a burning desire for wealth, is the only dependable means of accumulating wealth.**

You have to promise yourself that "I seek to keep myself free from consumer debt. I will spend less than I earn and regularly save or invest part of my income."

RULES OF MONEY: SPEND LESS THAN YOU EARN

WHY THE RICH GETS RICHER

<table>
<tr><td>THE POOR</td><td>THE RICH</td></tr>
</table>

"Never judge the future of a person based on their present conditions, because time has the power to change any black coal to a shiny diamond".

Chapter Five
Strategy

Financial Uneducated People Do

They go to Work → to Earn Income → to Buy Needs + Wants

What Financial Smart People Do

They go to Work → to Earn Income → to Save + Invest

What Financial Independent People Do

They enjoy life because they have Time and Freedom → They Earn Income → Build more Savings + Investments → that Create Money

Why the Rich Get Richer

Primarily their revenue is always in excess of their expenses. Their surplus gets credited for investments.

A review of the rich man's financial statement shows why the rich get richer. The assets column continues to grow and therefore, the income it produces grows with it. The result is that the rich get richer. The money invested in the purchase of assets works 24x7 hours and generates income without his presence, such as Rental income on properties and the value of properties is also increasing without his efforts, also Fixed and term deposits in a bank or value of bonds and shares.

Who is Middle Class and why do they Struggle?

That sector of the population strives to balance out their revenues and expenses to acquire the basic amenities of life such as good health, education and, owning a house.

The reason they have to play it safe. Their balance sheet is not balanced. Instead, they are loaded with liabilities and have no real assets that generate income. Typically, their only source of income is their Salary. Their livelihood becomes entirely dependent on their employer.

The poor and the middle-class work for money.

The rich have money to work for them.

The poor or Middle class don't work to make themselves rich. They work to make others rich.

The most important rule is to know the difference between an asset and a liability. **Once you understand the difference, concentrate your efforts on buying income-generating assets. That's the best way to get started on a path to becoming rich.** Keep doing that, and your asset column will grow. Keep liabilities and expenses down so more money is available to continue pouring into the asset column.

If a young couple would put more money into their asset column early on, their later years would be easier. Their assets would grow and would be available to help to meet their obligations when their children grow up.

Want to grow rich? Concentrate your efforts on buying income-producing Assets.

Keep liabilities and expenses low.

When there are enough assets to generate more than enough income to cover expenses, the balance is reinvested into assets. It will grow the assets column in the Balance Sheet which produces more income. The result is that the one who understands the difference between assets and liabilities gets richer.

An important distinction is that rich people spend the surplus, while the poor and middle class spend their resources to buy assets. The poor and middle class often buy items like Houses, Diamonds, and Jewelry because they want to look rich. They look rich, but in a reality, they just get deeper into debt on credit. Whereas the rich people, build their asset column first and then out of the income generated from the asset column buys their luxuries.

HOW TO BE RICH......AND TO BE RICHER

A 9 to 5 job would not make you Rich. To be rich, you have to be an entrepreneur.

There are five common skills common in all Rich Entrepreneurs: and by adopting this strategy, no one can stop you to be Rich

1. **Marketing** (Your marketing skill should be strong)

2. **Sales work** (Your sales skill should be strong)

3. **Management** (You should be focused on teamwork)

4. **Personal Finance** (Your personal finance should be strong)

5. **Fortune Vision** (You have to be a fortune visionary)

Focus on your sales increasing trend. Funding is only on the basis of your increasing sales trend.

How to start a business?

You don't build a business. You build people, then people build the business.

1.**Start with a proprietorship firm** (on the increasing trend of sale and profit convert it to:

2.**Partnership Firm** (on increasing the trend of sale and profit convert it to:

3.**Private Limited Company** (on the increasing trend of sale and profit convert it to:

4.**Public Limited Company and launch your IPO** (Equity Share in the market)

When your sales are in the increasing trend, the profit will automatically be increased. When profit is in an increasing trend, the value of equity shares will be increased which attracts the increasing trend of public funding. Your share price of Rs. 10 will automatically be increased to Rs.80. your wealth of 1crore will be increased to 80crore. Your public funding will be increased day by day so and your wealth.

Why do you have to change your business from a Proprietorship to a Public Limited Company?

1. For proper handling of your increasing sale and profit

2. Increasing need for Finance (Funding)

3. To reduce the tax burden

Rate of Taxes

1.Proprietorship 30%

2.Partnership..30%

3.Private Limited Company...........................25%

(up to total sales or receipt Rs.400 crore)

4.Company registered under **Start-up India**   0%

Having MSME certification

The Exception of Tax up to turnover of 100 crores

Only you have to focus on increasing your sale, money will come from every direction.

RULES OF MONEY: ALWAYS EARNED MONEY WORKS FOR YOU

"It does not matter how slowly you go as long as you do not stop."

Chapter Six
Means of Earning Money

Never stop working for your vision, because you never know when your early morning struggle will turn into overnight Success.

A nice car, A house, and A degree are the old status symbols. The ultimate aim is Freedom.

Time Freedom

Location Freedom

Financial Freedom

Freedom and Health are the new status symbols.

The biggest difference between money and time. You always know how much money you have, but you never know how much time you have.

The real story of life

	Time	Money	Energy
Childhood	Yes	No	Yes
Young	No	Yes	Yes
Old	Yes	Yes	No

Money and investing don't know Age. They know Drive, Execution, and Consistency.

It's never too late to start.

YOUR INCOME OPTIONS

You are not born to work for others for a lifetime.

This is almost a form of Slavery.

You were not here just to work, pay bills and then die.

You were born for much more than that.

There are four sectors of business that are evergreen forever.

    a) **Transport**

    b) **Food Industry**

    c) **Education Sector**

    d) **Medical**

1.   **JOB:** No matter what you earn, there's neither security nor freedom in having a job.

If you have a job, you are replaceable

And if you are replaceable, you are unpaid

Does not matter if you are highly qualified/having a degree

Become a Creator / Business owner & Become Irreplaceable

That's how you command a High Income

        There are even Highest Paying Jobs without Degree

        a. Photographer

        b. Politician

        c. Modeling / Acting

        d. Personal Trainer

        e. Dance Instructor

        f. Real Estate Agent

        g. Purchasing Agent

        h. Registered Nurse

i.   Graphic Designer

j.   Creative House Décor

k.   Web Developer

l.   Designer

m.   Professional You Tuber

n.   Professional Blogger

o.   Cabin Crew Member

p.   Commercial Pilot

q.   Radio / Video Jokey

r.   Stock Market Professionals

s.   Tourism Professionals

t.   Fashion / Interior Designing

u.   Transportation / Distribution Manager

v.   Detectives & Criminal Investigation

w.   Warehouse Supervisor

x.   Sales Representative

y.   Mechanics / Electrician / Plumber

z.   Make-up Artist

2.   SELF-EMPLOYMENT: Most people turn to self-employment in an effort to create more Security. And moreover to get more returns proportionate to their efforts

A.   Online Teaching

B.   Cook Food & Delivery

C.   Earn Money from Social- Media (Youtube)

D.   Sell your product online

E.   Online Part-time Job

3.   BUY A FRANCHISE: If you have a couple hundred thousand dollars to gamble, you can buy a good franchise. Marketing is not required for a good brand or Franchise. One of the biggest Franchise in India is "Amul" having more than 9000 outlet partners.

4.   INVESTMENTS: One should look beyond bank deposits now as rates of interest are declining by the day. And now even deposits into Banks are not safe because of the failure of most Banks and due to the slowdown of Govt. in the economy.

5.   BE A PROFESSIONAL: Successful authors, Writers, and Actors.

6.   NETWORK MARKETING: 21st Century Miracle Business. Become an Entrepreneur without any Risk. Networking means Time, Money & Security with Passive Income, and building relationships that give you the opportunity to ask for referrals. Asking for Referrals is about how you ask for business from people who are in your networks, including past clients and your sphere of influence.

The way products are marketed and distributed by replacing salaried middlemen and retailers with commission only. Today the cost of distribution and sales are about 80% to 90% included in the price of a product. By network marketing sales are conducted through person-to-person relationships and face-to-face interactions. Network Marketers are shaking hands and making friends and recruiting new independent business owners/partners.

Network Marketing is a multi-level pyramid. The company enters into partnerships with a network of independent distributors. The distributors' jobs are to move as much product as they can through an independent network of distributors.

Network Marketing companies pay their distributors so well in the form of commissions—instead of advertising widely in the media.

This is a marketing of compounding such as:

*Company employs 10 distributors   Total of 10

* Each of these 10 distributors employs a further 10   Total of 100

* Further each of these 100 distributors employs 10   Total of 1000

These numbers of distributors are compounding to 10000 and so on…

Now if the price of the product is Rs. 2000 the commission is 10% and 1% on every additional sale of each distributor included in this pyramid team. Suppose each distributor sold only one product, even though Commission will be paid to them:

The commission is growing as the distributors are increasing. This is the advantage of compounding income in this Networking Marketing.

Why Network Marketing is making more and more popular.

- Advertising is too expensive
- Distribution and sales costs are skyrocketing
- Consumers are demanding better customer service and shop-at-home convenience.

The best thing about Network Marketing is not that people are getting rich, it's that people are building rich lives in the process. Making money is nice, but having fun, making friends, and making a difference is priceless.

But there is a drawback to this type of business

1. Most companies are here to generate their wealth.

2. Their products are so much costly that they could not be sold in the open market.

3. They earn even 200% profit on their products whereas only 20 to 25% out of it they distribute as commission to their distributors.

4. Their products consist of a package of say about Rs.3000 to Rs.5000, which they have been forced to purchase.

5. They have products like of cosmetics, health (protein), toothpaste, cooking oils beauty soap and washing powder, etc.

6. In their seminars they show that their distributors are earning tons of commission.

7. They give awards to their high performers so that they include more and more in their networking chain.

"We live in a world
Where working 50 years for someone is normal
But working for yourself for even a year is considered risky."

RECAP

HOW TO EARN?

There are three types of income.

Earned Income

This is a primary income that is earned by our actions, it includes income earned from salary.

Investment Income

This income has no relation to the number of hours worked. It keeps on accruing over a period of time and is generated by selling investments that were made earlier.

Passive Income

This can be earned from rent, interest, or dividends. A person who is earning 25% of their income from passive sources is better off than a person who is earning 100% of their income in the form of a salary.

Everyone wants to be rich and wants to know a shortcut method to earn tons of money in a single shot. **You wouldn't plant a seed and then dig it up every few minutes to see if it has grown. Have patience, stop overthinking, and keep watering your seeds.** Fruits on a tree never grow in a day one has to care for and wait for a required period of time.

If you want to be rich, you need to be financially literate and know how to read financial statements.

The basic purpose to learn about financial management is to present a complete financial picture of the business with the help of two financial statements

Profit & Loss Account: shows the total Revenues & Expenses incurred during the accounting period.

Balance Sheet: the Balance Sheet is prepared to ascertain the true financial position of a business. It displays Assets and Liabilities.

Learn how to read the Cash Flow Statement

With the help of a cash flow statement, one can understand whether he is a rich, poor, or middle-class person.

FORMULA FOR EARNING MONEY

"Keep expenses low, reduce liabilities, purchase income-generating assets"

The best way to get started on a path to becoming rich. Keep doing that, and your asset column will grow. Keep liabilities and expenses down so more money is available to continue pouring into the asset column.

The most important rule is to know the difference between an asset and a liability. **Once you understand the difference, concentrate your efforts on buying income-generating assets. That's the best way to get started on a path to becoming rich.** Keep doing that, and your asset column will grow. Keep liabilities and expenses down so more money is available to continue pouring into the asset column.

A wealthy man is wealthy because of his Rich Thinking.

And a poor man is poor because of his poor Thinking.

Middle-Class purchase Property which never earns

House….40 Lakh

Car………20 Lakh

Mobile….1 Lakh

Rich People invest in Real Property which earns a regular income.

Mall…………..50 Lakh

Business……..30 Lakh

Shares……….10 Lakh

Money

Poor   Spend

Middle-class Save

Rich   Invest

Wealthy have most of their money stored in Business interests, Real Estate, and Managed assets.

The lower earners have most of their money stored in.

Homes, Cars, and Retirement Plans.

The Poor man is not the one who has zero bank balance, but the Poor man is the one who has no dream in his life.

The Rich gets richer because the Poor think every opportunity is a scam.

Stage-2
Save Money

HOW TO SAVE?

Money Speak

Money speaks only one language.

If you save me today, I will save you Tomorrow.

The source of income should be more than two

One income should be to pay for your needs and wants.

And the other income is for Investment.

It is mostly said that:

INCOME – EXPENSES = SAVING

But actually, it should be:

INCOME – SAVING = EXPENSES

We save basically because we can't predict the future. Saving money can help you become financially secure and provide safety in case of an emergency. Saving is an essential tool that will make your future financially stable. Saving money is one of the essential aspects of building wealth and having a secure financial future. Saving money gives you a way out from the uncertainties of life and provides you with an opportunity to enjoy a quality life.

Wealthy people have a great habit of saving money and controlling their expenses to grow wealth.

Here are a few benefits of savings which will help you understand the importance of saving money:

1. **Peace of mind**: When you are financially secure, you will get a good sleep because you know that you can be ready to face any uncertainties.

2. **Make you Retirement Ready**: Making a habit of saving some part of your income over several years can accumulate into a retirement fund, which makes your retirement more comfortable.

3. **Helps in emergencies**: You don't know what will happen to you the next minute. There will be pressure to look for extra funds on short notice.

4. **Money starts working for you**: If your savings are invested in the right place, your money starts working for you. You will earn interest on your Fixed deposits, dividends on your Mutual funds & on equity, and rent on your property in the money invested every year, which gets compounded and builds a vast corpus.

5. **Limits Debt**: This decreases and limits the amount of debt liability and also helps to avoid taking any emergency loan. Moreover, it also saves the amount that could have been spent on interest.

6. **Help to achieve your Dreams**: By setting a goal and saving money for the future will help to achieve your dreams.

7. **Financial Independence**: One of the best parts of life is being independent and having the freedom to do what you want.

Saving doesn't mean that you cut your needed expenses extremely. Rather avoid unnecessary expenses on purchases and on entertainment.

Tips for Saving Money

1. **Daily Saving**: Every day put all of your loose change into a money box and every month deposit it into your saving account.

2. **Recurring Deposit**: Try to open a Recurring deposit account in the Bank or in the Post office connected to your saving account and a fixed sum of money is automatically transferred to a recurring account from your saving account. You will be surprised that a huge sum of the amount will be collected due to the compounding interest of the recurring deposit. Compounding is the main base by which one can become a millionaire.

3. **Pay Yourself First**: If you pay yourself first before you pay your bills. This may be 10% of your paycheque or any amount you decide to save.

4. **Save the windfall income**: 1. Raises in Salary, 2. Bonus received, 3. Overtime wages, 4. Tax Refund from Income Tax,

It is suggested that people should save 10% to 15% of their income for retirement purposes. However, financial planners now consider this as outdated advice. This is because careers have become shorter, and the most obvious solution is to increase the amount of money that is saved for retirement so that there is enough money accumulated in the few years that they have until retirement.

"The only person standig in your way is you."

Chapter One
How Much Saving is Required for Retirement?

Retirement is at the age of 60 years and after that, you have to live up to 20 to 25 years without the help of a pension. A few things which I want to guide you are:

1. **If you have not saved** during your twenties, then now you have to save 30% to 50% of your income for the future.

2. **You should spend less** on your kids besides the expenses of their educations.

3. **You should invest** in Provident Fund or in any Pension Plan.

4. **If you have no house** of your own. Now at the age of 40 years, it's not good to take a home loan for a long period of time. Pay all your debts as soon as possible.

5. **Health is more important**. You have to buy health insurance for at least 5 lacs. And moreover, you have to take term insurance at least for one crore.

6. **You must have an emergency fund** with you. Buy at least 10 grams of Gold so that in any emergency you may sell it.

It is important for us to know the amount of money that will be required post-retirement. If a person does not change their lifestyle too much, and their expenditure does not change too much. The current expenses are then inflation-adjusted to reach the age of retirement.

Example: How much is saved for retirement?

For a person of 35 years of age

Monthly expenses are Rs. 20000/- pm

Annual expenses will be Rs.240000 (20000 x 12)

Retirement at the age of 60 years

Expected life 80 years

Expenses required for 20 years (80-60)

Money required to run a normal life after retirement Rs.48,00,000 (240000 x 20)

10% increase on account of inflation RS.52,80,000 (4800000 + 10%)

If a person invests Rs.52,80,000 on a minimum return of 5% annually

He will get Rs. Rs.264000 per year (5280000 x 5%)

6 TIPS TO SAVE

1. Reduce your Debts to Nil.

2. Don't purchase if it is not essential.

3. Take health insurance to save your saving.

4. Make sure that your saving is sufficient to beat inflation.

5. Use the law of compounding for investment to beat inflation.

6. Invest in Stock Market or Mutual Fund

Where to Save your Money

1. Public Provident Fund
2. National Saving Certificate
3. ELSS (Equity Linked Saving Scheme)
4. National Pension Scheme
5. ULIP
6. Life Insurance
7. Term Insurance
8. Deposit in Bank (Saving or Time deposit)
9. Deposit in Post Office (Saving or Time deposit)
10. Sukanya Samriddhi Yojana
11. Senior Citizens' Saving Scheme
12. Kisan Vikas Patra
13. Monthly Income Scheme
14. Recurring deposit
15. SIP of Mutual Funds

"Being rich is measured in dollars. Wealth is measured in time.

Most people think $1m cash is rich but if your expenses are $100k/month, your wealth is only 10 months.

The length of time you can survive without working is your true wealth.

Being rich is nice

Beingh wealthy is incredible."

Chapter Two
Managing Loans to Save Interest

How can you save Interest on Loans?

1. A personal loan at 9% may seem cheap but few customers realise that it is a flat- rate of interest. Every EMI reduces the principal outstanding whereas, on the flat rate the interest is not charged on the reduced balance of principal outstanding, it is always on the total amount of loan taken.

    The reduced rate of interest works out to almost 1.5 to 2 times the flat rate of interest depending on the tenure of the loan. Beware of these loan tricks.

    Don't fall for the flat rate of interest, here is how the rates can differ in a period of 5-year loan.

    - Flat rate is 9%
    - (if you add a 2% processing fee it will be 16.6%)
    - (if you pay two advances EMIs it will be 18%)
    - Reducing balance rate is 15.7%

    Fortunately, very few customers understand this math. Just showing a lower flat rate through this loan trick, the customer readily falls for it. For this, we should compare the EMI rather than the flat rate shown to us.

2. **Loan processing fee.** It is a small amount usually 1 to 2% of the loan amount with a cap of Rs.2000 to 3000, but these charges can increase the effective rate of the loan.

3. **Advance EMIs.** It is another invisible lever that can push up the effective interest rate. It is a simple arithmetical trick that reduces the net disbursed amount by getting the customer to pay two EMIs in advance. The EMI of a loan of Rs.5 lakh at 14% for two years comes to Rs.24000. If you pay two EMIs upfront, the net loan disbursed reduces to Rs.4.52 lakh, though you are charged for the full Rs.5 lakh.

    When taking loans, customers are usually so concerned about the disbursed amount that the payment of two EMIs doesn't bother them too much. It should be because the upfront payment of two EMIs pushes up the effective interest rate of the loan from 14% to 16.6%.

4. **Terms and Conditions of Loan.** They never let the customer read and understand the clauses in the loan document. The terms and conditions are any way printed in a very small font and customers are encouraged to quickly sign on the cross marked on each sheet of the loan agreement and get over with it. When you do that, you effectively sign away your right to challenge. For instance, the RBI has asked banks not to levy foreclosure charges on floating-rate loans but there is no such restriction on fixed-rate loans. But you wouldn't have read them if you were signing without reading.

5. **Insurance.** They have a commission on selling an insurance policy. This is a single-premium term plan with home loans. The policy covers the borrower and pays off the loan if something untoward happens to him. The

premium payable gets added to the loan- an amount so the customer doesn't have to pay from his pocket. This might sound very helpful but is not a good idea. Such policies are structured in a way that the death benefit progressively comes down as the borrower pays off the loan. A regular term plan with annual premium payments, even if slightly costlier, is a better idea than a single premium insurance cover linked to a loan. Besides, nobody tells the borrower about a key clause in such policies. If he forces to close the loan or shift to another lender, the insurance contract ends. However, this insurance can be purchased from elsewhere as well. A bank can't insist that the customer buys the insurance from it.

Five Tips for getting housing loan (5/20/30/40/50)

a. Loan should not be more than 5 times of your annual income.

b. Loan should not be more than 20 years.

c. EMI should not be more than 30% of your monthly income.

d. Housing Loan should not be taken after the age of 40 years.

e. Total EMI of all the loans should not be more than 50% of your monthly income.

RULES OF MONEY: KEEP YOUR FINANCE ORGANIZED

"It always seems impossible until it's done."

Chapter Three
Saving Through Creating A Personal Budget

Personal budgets are usually created to help an individual or a household of people to control their spending and achieve their financial goals. Having a budget can help people feel more in control of their finances and make it easier for them to not overspend and to save money. People who budget their money are less likely to obtain large debts and are more likely to be able to lead comfortable retired life and to be prepared for emergencies.

In the most basic form of creating a personal budget, the person needs to calculate their net-income track their spending over a set period of time, set goals based on the information previously gathered, make a plan to achieve their goals, and adjust their spending based on the plan. There exist many methods of budgeting to help people do this.

50/30/20 Budget

The 50/30/20 budget is a simple plan that sorts personal expenses into three categories: "needs" (basic necessities), "wants", and saving. 50% of one's net income then goes towards needs, 30% towards wants, and 20% towards savings.

Pay Yourself First Method (80/20 Budget)

In the pay-yourself-first budget people first save at least 20% of their net income, and then freely spend the remaining 80%.

They can also choose a 70/30, 60/40, or 50/50 budget for more savings. The most important part of this method is to put one's savings apart before spending on anything else.

Sub-Savings Accounts Method

This method is a variation of the pay-yourself-first budget, in which people create multiple savings accounts, each for one specific goal (such as a vacation or a new car), and each with an amount of money that should be reached by a specific date. They then divide the amount of money needed by the timeline to calculate how much they should save each month.

Monthly Budget Method

This seemingly innocuous exercise can be crucial in achieving financial goals, acquiring assets, or staying debt-free. Even so, many people find it hard to stick to a budget consistently in the long term. Here are some of the reasons why they are unable to maintain discipline and what they can do to ensure compliance.

There are several reasons you fail to be consistent with your monthly budget, says Riju Mehta

Even so, many people find it hard to stick to a budget consistently in the long term. Here are some of the reasons why they are unable to maintain discipline and what they can do to ensure compliance.

It is too unrealistic

Don't expect to save a large amount if you have a low income and all you spend are on needs, not wants.

What you should do

Set realistic targets. If you intend to save, you will need to track your expenses for a few months before deciding which ones you can cut. You will also have to discipline yourself about your spending consistently before you can increase your savings.

No spending discipline.

Big spenders find it especially hard to stick to a budget because they are unable to control the outgo, leaving them either with no money at the end of the month or unable to achieve their financial goals.

What you should do.

A good way to inculcate discipline is to fix your goals and automate savings. Once you know how much you need to save to reach your goals and the money goes out of your bank account as soon as your income arrives, it will be difficult to access money to spend. Importantly, get rid of your credit cards to curb the urge to spend.

Inaccuracies in tracking and record-keeping.

If you are not tracking every spend or forget to record it rigorously, you will not get a correct picture of your outgo and take wrong decisions or set unachievable goals.

What you should do.

Use a tracking and spending app, or simply keep a notebook to record your spending, and do it regularly. Fix a specified time each day or in a week to do so.

You don't have goals.

An easy way to justify your spending is that you have a lot of money lying in your account and you don't need it immediately.

What you should do.

Identify all your goals, big and small, and fix the goal values by taking into account inflation. Calculate the exact amount you will need after a specified time so that you know how much you need to save each month for every goal.

You are too strict.

If you cut out all of your, and your family's dispensable, fun spending like eating out or entertainment, you or your family will rebel sooner than later and kick out the budget.

What you should do.

Make a provision in the budget itself for light spending or occasional discretionary purchases like eating out to let off the steam of following a tight budget. It will keep you and your family motivated enough to stick to the budget.

The Family is not on board.

If you are saving, but your spouse cannot resist the urge to buy big-ticket gadgets, or the children insist on keeping up with their peers' spending styles, you alone will not be able to sustain it.

What you should do.

Talk to your family about what you are planning and how you intend to achieve it. The best way to keep every member motivated is to show them what saving can achieve a bigger house, a vacation abroad, foreign education, etc.

Your budget is static

A budget is not a static thing and will need to be changed with altered circumstances and life stages.

What you should do.

When the income rises, make fresh investments. If you face a salary cut, remove discretionary expenses. When you have a child include new goals and increase your savings. Make your budget evolve with every financial development.

You forget big annual expenses.

If you don't take into account the bigger expenses you are planning in the year, say, house painting and renovation or a longer holiday or buying a bigger home appliance or furniture, your budget will go haywire when you have to pay a large amount all at once.

What you should do.

When you review your budget at the start of the year, make sure to include the bigger financial expenses you are planning through the year. This will help you to calculate the extent of slashing your expenses require on a monthly basis so that you can save for the bigger expenses.

You don't have an emergency fund

One of the biggest stumbling blocks while trying to stick to a budget is dealing with eventualities for which you have made no monetary provision. So, if your house requires urgent repairs, or you face a sudden salary cut, or you fall ill and don't have sufficient insurance, your budget will go for a toss due to the big expenses.

What you should do.

Before you start work on your budget build an emergency fund that is equal to 3-6 months' household expenses. In addition to this either buy health insurance or keep a substantial buffer to take care of your medical expenses.

Monthly Budget Statement	Monthly Expenditure
Food	Rs.
Clothing	Rs.
Household Maintenance	Rs.
Rent / Home Loan Payment	Rs.
Car / Bike Loan Payment	Rs.

Car / Bike Maintenance	Rs.
Transportation (Fuel, Fares)	Rs.
Utilities (Electricity / Water)	Rs.
Child Care	Rs.
Personal Care	Rs.
Insurance	Rs.
Credit Card Payment	Rs.
Income Tax	Rs.
Property Tax	Rs.
Dues	Rs.
Retirement Plan Investments	Rs.
Saving / Investing	Rs.
Contributions	Rs.
Entertainment	Rs.
Others	Rs.
Total Monthly Expenditure	Rs.
MONTHLY RECEIPT	
Salary / Wages	Rs.
Interest (FDs, Savings A/cs	Rs.
Dividends (M.Fund, Stocks etc.)	Rs.
Rental or Royalty	Rs.
Others	Rs.
Total Monthly Receipts	Rs.
NET CASH FLOW	
Total Monthly Receipts	Rs.
Total Monthly Expenditure	Rs.
Monthly Net Cash Flow	Rs.

Chapter Four
Managing Taxes to Save Income

Taxes also reduces our income: if we understand the law of Taxes. We can save more out of our income. If we understand to save our Tax liabilities, we can save more to increase our income-generating assets. We have more funds in our hands to invest.

One who is an employee or small business sole proprietor understands the tax advantages and protection provided by a Government/ Corporation to save on funds more efficiently.

The Law (Income Tax & Other Taxes)

Taxes form a major source of revenue for the Government. There are two types-Direct taxes income-tax and Indirect taxes like Customs duty, GST (goods & service tax), etc. Among the direct taxes, Income-tax assumes great significance since it affects directly individuals-the layman.

True capitalists used their financial knowledge to simply find an escape. Rich people do not work individually. They do work under a registered company, a legal body without a soul. Using it the wealth of the rich is once again protected. People with high financial IQ learn to use others' money to become rich.

The income tax rate of a corporation is less than the individual income tax rate. In addition, certain expenses could be claimed by a corporate with pre-tax. They search for ways to minimize their tax burden. They hire smart accountants and persuade politicians to change laws or create legal loopholes. They use their resources to effect change.

Saving through Tax Planning

HOW YOU CAN SAVE YOUR TAX WITHOUT INVESTING

Permissible deductions from Salary

1.Standard Deduction

Tax benefit u/s 16(ia)

Savings: Rs.50000

A standard deduction of Rs.50000 or the amount of salary, whichever is less, shall be allowed.

2.Tax Rebate for Small Taxpayers

Tax benefit u/s 87A

Savings: Rs.12500

A resident individual having a total income of up to Rs.5 lakh shall be entitled to a tax rebate from his income-tax liability. The amount of rebate shall be equal to the amount of income-tax payable or Rs.12500, whichever is less.

3.House Rent Allowance

Tax benefit u/s 10(13A), 80GG

Saving: Rs.60000

Any assessee including an employee who is not in receipt of H.R.A u/s 10(13A) or a self-employed person. A deduction is allowable in respect of rent paid by an assessee for his residential accommodation. The assessee, his spouse, does not own any residential house at the place of his employment.

Amount of Deduction: At least of the following amounts is allowable

  (i)   Rent paid minus 10% of the assessee's total income; or

  (ii) Rs.5000 p.m.; or

  (iii) 25% of total income

4.Deduction in respect of LIC Premium, NSC, PPF, Home loan repayment, Tuition Fee of two children

Tax benefit u/s 80C

Saving: Rs.150000

The deduction is allowed for the amount paid or deposited by the assessee in the specified schemes, subject to a maximum of Rs.150000

Specified Schemes: 1. Life Insurance Premium, 2. Contribution to Provident Funds, 3. Saving in National Savings Certificates, 4. Subscription to any Mutual Fund u/s 10(23D), 5. Tuition fees to any educational institution situated in India for the purpose of full-time education of any two children, 6. Amount paid for Housing Loan Instalment and stamp duty, registration fee, and other expenses paid for transfer or the purchase of a residential house. 7. Term deposit for a fixed period of at least 5 years. 8. Subscription to notified bonds issued by the National Bank for Agriculture and Rural Development.

5. Deduct the amount of Medical Insurance.

Tax benefit u/s 80D

Saving: Rs.25000 to Rs.50000 (Aggregate deduction shall not exceed Rs.50000)

The deduction is allowed for medical insurance (Mediclaim) premiums or contributions to Central Govt. Health Scheme (CGHS) or payment for preventive health check-ups, for self or family, subject to a maximum of Rs.25000.

Deduct the amount of medical treatment expenditure in respect of self or family member (being a senior citizen, not having Mediclaim cover), subject to a maximum of Rs.50000

6. Deduction of interest on the loan for higher education.

Tax benefit u/s 80E

Saving: without any limit

The deduction in the amount paid to a financial institution or approved charitable institution, towards interest on a loan taken for higher education, without any limit.

7. Deduction from Income from Properties

Tax benefit u/s 24

Saving: 30% of the net annual value of the property

   a)   **Let-out Properties**

Standard Deduction: Standard deduction of 30% of the net annual value of the property

Interest on Borrowed Capital: Interest payable in India on borrowed capital, where the property has been acquired, constructed, repaired, renovated, or reconstructed with such borrowed capital is allowable (without any limit)

8. Deduction of the interest on the loan for an affordable house.

Tax benefit u/s 80EEA

Saving: Rs.150000

Deduction of the amount of interest on loan taken (during 1/4/2019 to 31/3/2021) for residential house property, under affordable housing scheme, subject to a maximum of Rs.150000

9. Deduction of the interest on the loan for the purchase of an Electric Vehicle.

Tax benefit: u/s 80EEB

Saving: Rs.150000

Deduction of the amount of interest on loan taken (from 1/4/2019 to 31/3/2023) for purchasing an Electric Vehicle, subject to a maximum of Rs.150000

Tax Liability and Rebate under New Tax Regime

The new tax regime shall apply in relation to A.Y.2021-22 and subsequent years.

The assesses shall have the option to pay tax under the old tax regime at the applicable rates of tax claiming all available exemptions and deductions, or under the new tax regime availing concessional rates of tax and only limited exemptions and deductions.

For A.Y. 2024-25

Standard deduction from Salary/Pension / Family Pension is allowable under new tax regime also.

A resident individual shall be entitled to a tax rebate equal to an amount as under:

1. If total income is up to Rs.7 lacs

    Amount of income-tax payable (before allowing any rebate / relief) or

    Rs.25000, whichever is less.

    (Income tax Rs.25000 on Taxable Income of Rs.700000)

2. If total income exceeds Rs.7 lacs.

    Marginal relief shall be allowed i.e., amount of income-tax payable

    (before allowing any rebate/ relief) – (Total income – Rs.7 lacs)

Chapter Five
How Your Family Can Help You Save Tax

Here is how you can invest, insure and save through your Parents, Spouse, and Children in a way that reduces your tax liability.

PARENTS

1.Invest in their name by gifting them money. This amount will not be taxable

Tax benefit u/s 80TTB Rs.50000 of interest income is exempt.

The tax-exempt limit for senior citizens above 60 years, is Rs.3 lakh, and for very senior citizens above 80 years, it is Rs.5 lakh.

This money can be invested in the Senior Citizens' Saving Scheme, Post office, or other tax-saving schemes, even in fixed deposits.

Senior Citizens are allowed tax exemption of up to Rs.50000 on the interest income from saving or fixed deposit in any bank, post office, or cooperative bank, as opposed to Rs.10000 for those below 60 years. Even if the interest exceeds the exemption limit, they will pay a much lower tax than you.

2.Pay Rent to Parents

Tax benefit U/S 10(13A)

Savings: The least of the three

    i.   **Actual rent paid minus 10% of basic salary**

    ii. **Total HRA that the employer paid**

    iii. **40-50% of the basic salary depending on residential conditions.**

If you are a salaried employee and staying with your parents in a house owned by them and not co-owned by you, you could pay the rent and claim HRA exemption, it will be beneficial if they fall in the tax-exempt income limit or a lower tax bracket than you.

While this amount will be taxable in their hands, they can claim a deduction of 30% of the annual rent for repairs and maintenance u/s 24. Also remember, that if the rent is above Rs.1 lakh a year, their PAN Card details will have to be shared.

3.Buy Health Insurance

Tax benefit u/s 80D

Savings up to Rs.25000 to Rs.50000

If you buy health insurance for your senior citizen parents, who are above 60 years of age, you can claim a tax deduction of up to Rs.50000 for the premium paid. For parents below 60 years of age, this amount is Rs.25000.

SPOUSE

1.Take a Joint Home Loan

Tax benefit u/s 80C for principal amount & u/s 24 for interest on loan

Saving up to Rs.7 lakh (depending on the amount of loan taken)

Up to Rs.3 lakh for principal repaid (R.1.5 lakh each) + Rs.4 lakh for interest repaid (Rs.2 lakh each)

For husband and wife who are co-borrowers and co-owners of a self-occupied property, each can claim a tax benefit on interest and principal paid for a home loan.

2.Give a Loan

Savings: If for instance, you give a loan of Rs.2 lakh to your wife at 6% interest and she puts it in an equity mutual fund giving 10% return, the capital gain of less than Rs.1 lakh in a year will be tax-free.

If you gift money to your wife and it is invested, the income will be clubbed with your income and taxed unless you choose a tax-free instrument like the PPF. Instead, you can give a loan to the spouse who has no or low income, at a reasonable rate of interest. Though the interest will be added to your income and taxed, you will be able to save if she invests in an instrument with a higher rate of return.

3.Education Loan

Tax benefit u/s 80E

Savings: If, for instance, your gross taxable income after all deductions is Rs.7 lakh and you repay Rs.2 lakh as

the interest component of the loan, your taxable income would be R.5 lakh. And there is a tax exemption up to the taxable income of Rs.5 lakh.

If you have taken an education loan for your spouse for higher studies, you will get tax benefits on repayment of interest for up to 8 years starting from the year in which interest payment begins. The loan has to be from any financial institution approved by the government.

CHILDREN

1.Invest for a child in PPF, Mutual Fund, Ulips, and Insurance

Tax benefit u/s 80C

Savings: Up to Rs.1.5 lakh

You can also invest in equity mutual funds as there is no tax if the gain is less than Rs.1 lakh a year.

2.Education Loan

Tax benefit u/s 80E

Savings: If, for instance, your gross taxable income after all deductions is Rs.7 lakh and you repay Rs.2 lakh as the interest component of the loan, your taxable income would be R.5 lakh. And there is a tax exemption up to the taxable income of Rs.5 lakh.

If you have taken an education loan for your child for higher studies, you will get tax benefits on repayment of interest for up to 8 years starting from the year in which interest payment begins. The loan has to be from any financial institution approved by the government.

3.Open a bank savings account

Tax benefit u/s 10(32)

Saving: Up to Rs.1500 per child for two kids will be tax-exempt.

In fact, any income will be entitled to an exemption of Rs.1500 a year

4.Pay tuition fee /education allowance /hostel expenses

Tax benefit u/s 80C & U/S 10

Savings: Rs.2400 + Rs.7200 a year (u/s 10)

Under section 80C you can include the tuition fee paid for a maximum of two children each year. If you are a salaried employee, you can also claim an exemption of Rs.100 per month, per child up to two kids, as children's education allowance and Rs.300 a month, per child as hostel expenditure allowance. If the assessee has paid the tuition fee for his own studies, he will not be eligible for deduction u/s 80C. In other words tuition fee paid for self-education is not allowable

5.Buy health insurance

Tax benefit u/s 80D

Savings up to Rs.25000 (including medical check-ups of Rs.5000

If you are paying the premium for health insurance for your spouse and children, it will be entitled to tax exemption, it also includes any preventive health check-ups.

6.Deduction for a dependant with a disability, disease

Tax benefit u/s 80DDB

Savings

If the dependant is less than 60 years of age and suffers from a specific disease, you can claim a deduction of Rs.40000, or actual expenses, whichever is lesser. If the person is 60 years or above, you can claim Rs. One lakh, or actual expenses, whichever is lesser. In the case of disability, if it is between 40-80%, you can claim a maximum deduction of Rs.75000. If the disability is more than 80%, the available deduction is Rs.1.25 lakh

DOUBLE TAXATION RELIEF

Double taxation of income arises when a resident taxpayer derives income from a source in another country or specified territory outside India and such income is charged to tax in both the countries i.e. country of residence of the tax-payer as well as in the country of the source of income.

For avoidance of such double taxation of income and grant of relief. India has entered into agreements with certain foreign countries. Such Double Taxation Avoidance Agreements (DTAA)

Relief wehere no DTA Agreement Exists

If a person resident in India proves that tax has been paid in respect of his income which accrued or arose to him during the relevant financial year in the countries with which India has no DTA Agreement, he shall be granted unilateral double taxation relief, by way of a deduction, from the India income tax payable by him, of an amount calculated on such doubly-taxed income at the Indian rate of tax or the rate of tax of the other country, whichever is lower. (Sec. 91)

How to calculate the Double Taxation Relief?

- Average Rate of Indian Tax
- Average Rate of Foreign Tax
- Relief Whichever is lower

Example :

COMPUTATION OF TAXABLE INCOME

	Amount
INCOME FROM INDIA	374000
INCOME FROM FOREIGN	500000
Gross Taxable Income	**874000**
Less: Deduction u/s 80c,80D,80TT,80CC	300000
Net Taxable Income	**574000**
Income Tax Payble	27300
Less: Rebate u/s 87A	**0**
Income Tax	**27300**
Edu.cess @4%	**1092**
Tax Payble	**28392**

Average Tax India

$$\frac{28392 \times 100}{574000} = 4.95\%$$

Average Tax Foreign = 4.94%

Out of two 4.94 % is less

Less: Relief u/s 90 (500000x4.94%)   -24700

Tax Payble in India   3692

Chapter Six
Tax Saving Schemes

Post Office Deposits

1. **Sukanya Samriddhi Yojana**

   Minimum / Maximum Investment......Rs.250 / Rs.1.50 lakh p.a.

   One account per girl child

   Tax benefits (Sec.80C)

2. **Senior Citizen's Savings Scheme**

   Minimum / Maximum Investment......Rs.1000 / Rs.30 lakh

   5year tenure, minimum age 60 yrs.

   Tax benefits (Sec.80C)

3. **Public Provident Fund**

   Minimum / Maximum Investment......Rs.500 / Rs.1.50 lakh p.a.

   15-year tenure, tax-free returns

   Tax benefits (Sec.80C)

4. **5-year NSC VIII Issue**

   Minimum / Maximum Investment......Rs.1000 / No limit

   No TDS

   Tax benefits (Sec.80C)

5. Time Deposit

Minimum / Maximum Investment……Rs.1000 / No limit

5year tenures

Tax benefits (Sec.80C)

OTHER TAX-SAVING SCHEMES

6. Life Insurance Policy

Tax benefits (Sec.80C)

7. Medical Insurance Policy

Tax benefits (Sec.80D)

Tax Planning of Retirement Benefits

1.Invest the amount received on retirement benefits or received under a voluntary retirement scheme / special voluntary retirement scheme, in the Senior Citizens Savings Scheme, 2004, carrying interest @8% p.a. (taxable).

2.Invest the retirement benefits in monthly income schemes such as:

a. Annuity plans of LIC. Investment is eligible for deduction u/s 80 C.

b. 5-year Post Office Monthly Income Scheme.

3.Do not withdraw from the Provident Fund account immediately, if interest is available even after retirement, as interest on the provident fund is exempt under Income Tax.

These are the Six Financial Services you need to start today.

1. Make a Monthly Budget
2. Live life according to the money you have
3. Pay off your bills on time

4.   Avoid taking loans
5.   Build your own emergency fund
6.   Plan for your Retirement

Do not save what is left after spending, instead spend what is left after saving… Warren Buffett

"You can always make more money,
But you can never get back time."

RECAP

HOW TO SAVE?

Saving is an essential tool that will make your future financially stable. Saving money is one of the essential aspects of building wealth and having a secure financial future.

It is suggested that people should save 10% to 15% of their income for retirement purposes.

It is mostly said that:

INCOME – EXPENSES = SAVING

But actually, it should be:

INCOME – SAVING = EXPENSES

Retirement is at the age of 60 years and after that, you have to live up to 20 to 25 years without the help of a pension.

How you can save interest on loan

Don't fall for the flat rate of interest, here is how the rates can differ in a period of a 5-year loan.

- Flat rate is 9%
- (if you add a 2% processing fee it will be 16.6%)
- (if you pay two advances EMIs it will be 18%)
- Reducing balance rate is 15.7%

Personal budgets are usually created to help an individual or a household of people to control their spending and achieve their financial goals. Having a budget can help people feel more in control of their finances and make it easier for them to not overspend and to save money.

We can save more out of our income. If we understand to save our Tax liabilities, we can save more to increase our income-generating assets. We have more funds in our hands to invest.

These are the Six Financial Services you need to start today.
1. Make a Monthly Budget
2. Live life according to the money you have
3. Pay off your bills on time
4. Avoid taking loans
5. Build your own emergency fund
6. Plan for your Retirement

Stage-3
Invest Money

HOW TO INVEST?

What is Investment?

Usain Bolt won 8 Gold Medals in 3 Olympics, and he only Ran for less than 115 seconds on the Track Earning $ 119 Million Dollars.

That is the Economy of Effort

But for those 2 minutes, he trained for 20 years. That is Investment.

Think Long Term, Patience Pays.

When you Invest, you are buying a day that you don't have to Work. "Aya Laraya"

Investment takes our savings for making money and puts it into financial instruments or products such as shares, bonds, property, and even term deposits. Investment generates income and may also increase in value over time. Your investments can make your good times better and help you in your bad times.

Top Reasons to Invest

- Protect Your Purchasing Power.
- Grow Your Capital.
- Achieve Your Financial Goals.

- Earn More Than Earn a Savings Account.
- Diversify Your Income.
- Save for Retirement.
- Lower Taxable Income.

WHY INVEST

1. **Financial security**: People want to be financially secure to meet unforeseen events.

2. **Financial independence**: It ensures that you have enough money to pay for your needs and wants for the rest of your life without having to rely on someone else or have to work in your old age.

3. **Building of wealth**: People invest with the view to build their wealth.

4. **Attaining goals**: Some people set a specific goal in life to be millionaire or billionaire and invest to achieve those goals. The goal you set would be your motivation to invest.

Be aware that before investing, you must understand that different investment choices have different risks.

TIPS TO INVEST

1. Reinvest income you earned from your investments

2. Invest at a good interest rate or with a company that is performing well and paying good dividends

3. As a general rule, investments with high returns tend to be riskier. Therefore, the appropriate risk for you depends on how much risk you are prepared to take.

4. Diversify your investment, don't put all your eggs in one basket. Put your money into a variety of investments to minimize your risks/losses of investing.

6 EXCELLENT TIPS BY WARREN BUFFETT

1. Never depend on a single income. Make investments to create a second source.

2. Don't put all your eggs in one basket.

3. Never test the depth of the river with both feet.

4. Do not save what is left after spending but spend what is left after saving.

If you want to be wealthy?

Don't Save Your Money Invest it

You can't physically work 24/7, But your money can.

If you don't find a way to make money while you sleep, you will work until you Die….Warren Buffett

"If your dream is to become successful in life,
Then you are the only one who has to pay the price for it.
No one else won't do it for you.
Keep this in mind."

Chapter One
Developing Investment Habits

Put your money to work

You cannot get rich with the money in your savings account

You must invest it in appreciating assets, Business, Real Estate, or in Stocks

HABITS: The general absence of ambition to be, to do, and to own. Fear of criticism, failure to create plans and to put them into action, because of what other people will think, People, refuse to take chances in business because they fear the criticism which may follow if they fail. The fear of criticism, in such cases, is stronger than the DESIRE for success.

You are a creator of habit. Habit is the function of your subconscious mind. If you repeat a negative thought or act over a period of time, you will be under the compulsion of a habit.

One of Henry Ford's most outstanding qualities is his-habit of reaching decisions quickly and definitely and changing them slowly.

The majority of people who fail to accumulate money sufficient for their needs are generally, easily influenced by the "opinions" of others. They permit the newspapers and the "gossiping" neighbors to do their "thinking" for them. "Opinions are the cheapest commodities on earth. If you are influenced by "opinions" when you reach DECISIONS, you will not succeed in any undertaking, much less in that of transmuting YOUR OWN DESIRE into money.

Tiny Habits for Big Results

Consistent, daily practice is how you make that happen. If you watered the plants just a little each day, over time your garden always grew.

Why do some people succeed at saving while others do not? Or, if they do save, it's not much more than whatever they are forced to do through EPF or NPS or tax-saving, etc. They never make the choice of saving.

Investing is not a choice in the normal sense but a matter of habit. The book "Tiny Habits" goes deep and yet easily into the process of conscious habit formation. The writer of this book "Fogg" says **that there are three ways to change behaviour. With one sudden realization, change the environment, or create tiny habits.** However, it is well understood by those who do not save that all you have to do is to make a beginning. The ideal first habit to form is to start investing a small regular amount through Recurring deposits or SIP. To those who haven't done it, it's hard to believe how change builds upon change and how behaviour changes. Tiny Habits can help.

"What is the hardest thing to break?
Surprisingly the answer
Is: HABIT
If you break the H, you still have 'A BIT'
If you break the 'A' you still have 'BIT'
If you break the 'B' you still have 'IT'
Even after you break the 'T' in IT, there is still 'I'
And that (I) is the root cause of all problems."

Chapter Two
Power of Compounding

MAGIC OF COMPOUND INTEREST

The seven wonders of the world are known globally today. But decades ago, Einstein regarded compound interest as the eighth wonder of the world.

Understanding compound interest

Compound interest means you not only earn returns on the principal money that you invest but also get to enjoy a return on the interest income that keeps adding to your principal. This process continues until you withdraw your money. In simple terms, with compound interest, you can grow your wealth by just staying put in your investments.

1. Benefit of compounding

    Invest Rs.2500/-pm

    Rate of interest @ 8% PA

    The duration of investment is 5 years

    Total investment amount Rs 1.5 Lakhs

    You will get Rs.1.85 Lakhs after 5 years

    Profit Rs.35 thousand

2. Benefit of compounding

    Invest Rs.2500/-pm

Rate of interest @ 8% PA

The duration of investment is 10 years

Total investment amount Rs 3 Lakhs

You will get Rs.4.6 Lakhs after 10 years

Profit Rs.1.60 Lakh

We can see the power of compounding for the long term in the return of PPF (Public Provident Fund) and of NPS (National Pension Scheme).

PPF (Public Provident Fund) is backed by the Government with a floating rate of 7.1% compounded on an annual basis.

Investors invest Rs.1.5 Lakhs annually for 15 years regularly @7.1% (assuming the rate is 7.1% throughout the tenure)

Investor deposits in 15 years Rs.22,50,000 and gets Rs.43 Lakhs

If the investor extends the period to 25 years, he will get Rs.1 crore while paying only Rs.37,50,000 in 25 years.

NPS (National Pension Scheme) Market linked scheme

Investors invest R.1.5 Lakhs annually for 13.5 years regularly at a conservative assumed return of 10% in NPS on maturity the sum will be Rs.1 crore approximately. And after 25 years it will be Rs.1.67 crore.

How does compounding work?

Let's take an example of A and B with their own unique investment strategies, here's how much they accumulated at the end of 10 years

To illustrate how compounding works, suppose Rs.100000 is held in an account that pays 10% interest annually. After the first year or compounding period, the total in the account has risen to Rs.110000, a simple reflection of Rs.10000 in interest being added to the Rs.100000 principal. In year two, the account realizes 10% growth on both the original principal and the Rs.10000 of first-year interest, resulting in a second-year gain of Rs.11000 and a balance of Rs.121000.

OPTED FOR REINVESTMENT OF INTEREST INVESTMENT OF A WITH COMPOUNDING

Year	Pricipal Money	Reinvest Money	Interest @10 P A	Total At The end of the Year
1.	100000		10000	110000
2.		110000	11000	121000
3.		121000	12100	133100
4.		133100	13310	146410
5.		146410	14641	161051
6.		161051	16105	177156
7.		177156	17716	194872
8.		194872	19487	214359
9.		214359	21436	235795
10.		235795	23580	259375
INTEREST INCOME			**159375**	
INTEREST RATE			**15.94%**	

OPTED FOR PAYOUT OF INTEREST
INVESTMENT OF B WITHOUT COMPOUNDING

Pricipal Money	Reinvest Money	Interest @10 P A	Yearly Payout
100000	100000	10000	10000
	100000	10000	10000
	100000	10000	10000
	100000	10000	10000
	100000	10000	10000
	100000	10000	10000
	100000	10000	10000
	100000	10000	10000
	100000	10000	10000
	100000	10000	10000
INTEREST INCOME	100000		
INTEREST RATE	**10%**		

Rs.100000 Investment Earning 10% Compounded Interest

After 10 years, assuming no withdrawals and a steady 10% interest rate, the account would grow to Rs.259375. Without having added or removed anything from our principal balance except for interest, the impact of compounding has increased the change in balance from Rs.10000 in Period 1 to Rs.159375 in Period 10.

In addition, without having added new investment on our own, our investment has grown Rs.259375 in 10 years. Had the investment only paid simple interest (10% on the original investment only), annual interest would have only been Rs.100000 (Rs.10000 per year for 10 years).

What do you need to do to benefit from the power of compounding?

1. **SAVE MORE:**

    To start investing, you first need to develop the habit of saving. This, in turn, calls for monitoring your expenses.

2. **START EARLY:**

    The power of compounding needs time to work its magic on your money. You must, thus, start investing as early as you can.

3. **BE PATIENT:**

    You can't expect immediate growth. To savor the benefits of compounding. You must think long-term and stay calm during market volatility.

4. **INVEST REGULARLY:**

    You must make regular investments to accelerate your wealth creation process. Mutual Fund Systematic Investment Plans can help you make periodic investments.

On the same principle, your small investment per month in recurring deposits converts into a huge amount.

"Big dreams requires big efforts

There is no compromise in that.

You will get on the basis of what you have paid

(In terms of hardwork)"

Chapter Three
Business As a Concept

First Rule of Business: Find a need and fulfill it.

"Your time is limited, so don't waste it living someone else's life." -Steve Jobs

Passion: Often, the combination of freedom and value comes about when someone takes action on something he or she loves to do anyway: a hobby, skill, or passion that person ends up transforming into a business model. Successful small businesses are often built on the pursuit of a personal hobby or interest. Most important merge your passion and skill with something that is useful to other people.

1.**When you are living a life of passion and obsession, there are no limits**. There are no time clocks or time off, no vacations and no bosses breathing down your neck to perform because with obsession, there is no boss, there is only you.

2.**If you stay true to yourself and your passion**, eventually you will find yourself doing exactly what you want to be doing if you remain persistent and true to your vision of your future and career.

3.**If you remain curious**, there's a better chance that you will eventually discover your passion.

4. **Sometimes passion only emerges from effort**. The effort at your job, effort as a spouse and a parent, effort in your hobbies and interests.

I remember one of my school- teachers. He loved to do the business of spectacles. Once he learned it from his father but due to a shortage of funds, he was not in a position to start the business. He used to visit our home for my tuition. Once he told my father about his passion to start a shop to sell spectacles. My father gave him a full-year tuition fee as support to start his business. He left his job as a teacher and with a small investment, he started his shop. It was his Passion or Skill+ Usefulness (People's demand) makes him a successful businessman. Now he is the owner of a big showroom of spectacles.

The goal of business is profit. There's nothing wrong with having a hobby, but if you want to call it a business, you have to make money. There are two important things to understand.

1.   **Spend as little money as possible to start your project**

2.   **Make as much money as you can.**

If your business focuses on giving people more of what they want, you are on the right track.

Your success in business depends upon three principles:

1.Product or service: what you sell

2.People willing to pay for it

3. Sell What People Buy

A better way is to give people what they actually want. Make what you want to buy yourself, and other people will probably want it too.

Within a period of 12 years, the turnover of PATANJALI (Popular for Ayurveda products) has reached more than 25000 crores whereas the turnover of a 100-year-old company (Baidyanath) is on the same business line is even less than 1000 crore. How PATANJALI has reached this height within a period of 12 years.

> 1. They used the name Ayurveda in the production of their products.

> 2. They are producing the products of daily use, what the people actually want.

> 3. Daily use products: Their turnover reached this level because of 6 products only, these Are: Cow Gee, Dant Kanti Toothpaste, Kesh Kanti Hair-oil & Shampoo, Herbal Beauty & Washing Powder Soap and Ayurveda Medicines.

Whereas the other companies are still making Ayurveda medicines which are not liked by everyone.

If you know what you need to do. Stop waiting. Start taking action. If you focus 100 percent on creating a quality product, you will rise to the top every time.

Putting the focus on income and cash flow ensures that a business remains healthy. You have to make sure that your recurring activities are directly tied to making maximum money as possible.

Once you have your vision, the fog lifts and your road map starts to become clear again. But nobody is going to drive the car for you. You have got to put in the work to achieve your goals and change your own life.

"A strong passion for any object will ensure success, for the desire of the end will point out the means" (Willian Hazlitt)

PERSISTENCE

Persistence is an essential factor in the procedure of transmuting DESIRE into its monetary equivalent. **The basis of persistence is the POWER OF WILL.** Will-power and desire, when properly combined, make an irresistible pair. There are four simple steps that lead to the Habit of PERSISTENCE. They call for no great amount of intelligence, no particular type of education, and little time or effort. **These four steps as a matter of habit are essential for success in all walks of life. necessary steps are:**

1.A definite purpose backed by a burning desire for its fulfillment.

2.A definite plan. Expressed in continuous action.

3. A mind closed tightly against all negative and discouraging influences. Including negative suggestions from relatives, friends, and acquaintances.

4. A friendly alliance with one or more persons who will encourage one to follow through with both plan and purpose.

"Nothing will work unless you do."- Maya Angelou

"Most of the time it happens that, the decision or move that we are afraid to take could be the one that changes everything in our life.

Our financial condition, emotional state, and spiritual awakening."

Chapter Four

Possible Blockades to Acquiring Fortune

Learn new skills and improve upon your existing ones.

Nothing will change your life faster than building new skills. Whatever the case, imagine a year where you start out having a limited skill set.

Dedicate time during your day to build your skills. Learn them via business books, and videos but don't forget to physically practice your skills too.

MAJOR CAUSES OF FAILURE: A few points were selected from the book. (Think and Grow Rich")

1. **Lack of a well-defined purpose in life**: There is no hope of success for the person who does not have a central purpose or definite goal at which to aim.

2. **Insufficient education**: Half-knowledge means wrong decision-making.

3. **Procrastination:** Waiting for the "time to be right" to start doing something worthwhile. Do not wait. The time will never be "just right." Start where you stand, and work with whatever tools you may have at your command, and better tools will be found as you go along.

4. **Negative personality**: A negative personality will not induce cooperation.

5. **Uncontrolled desire**. The gambling instinct drives millions of people to failure.

6. **Superstition and Prejudice**: A superstition is a form of fear and a sign of ignorance. Men who succeed keep open minds and are afraid of nothing.

7. **Inability to cooperate with others**: Friendly and cooperative relations with like-minded business friends.

8. **Intentional Dishonesty**: There is no substitute for honesty. There is NO HOPE for the person who is dishonest by choice. Sooner or later, his deeds will catch up with him, and he will pay by loss of reputation, and perhaps even loss of liberty.

9. **Guessing instead of thinking**: Most people are too indifferent or lazy to acquire FACTS with which to THINK ACCURATELY. They prefer to act on "Opinions" created by guesswork or snap judgments.

10. **Lack of Capital.** Lack of sufficient funds often results in loss of business opportunities.

You should know your weaknesses and strength. If you are influenced by the opinions of others, you will have no DESIRE of your own. You have a brain and mind of your own. Use it and reach your own decisions. Keep your eyes and ears wide open and your mouth CLOSED if you wish to acquire the habit of prompt DECISION.

Keep in mind the fact that every person with whom you associate is, like yourself, seeking the opportunity to accumulate money. If you talk about your plans too freely, you may be surprised when you learn that some other person has beaten you to your goal by PUTTING INTO ACTION AHEAD OF YOU, the plans of which you talked unwisely.

Let one of your first decisions be to KEEP A CLOSED MOUTH AND OPEN EARS AND EYES.

Chapter Five
Where to Invest?

**"It is a rough road that leads to the heights of greatness."
(Seneca)**

Don't buy a car until you Invest in some assets.

Most people think that just because you have money, you need to have a car.

Invest into some assets that will make you enough money to buy a car 10x over.

That is what the financially literate do when they have the ability to be wise with their money.

Investment takes your savings and makes your money work for you by putting it in financial instruments or products such as shares, bonds, property, and even term deposits. Investments generate income for you. You may receive dividends if you invest in shares, interest from term deposits, or rent from a property that you lease out.

There are varying reasons why people invest.

1. People want to be financially secure, and this is why they need to have extra money.

2. Investment enables you to be independent and not rely on the money of others to pay for your needs even in your old age.

3. People invest with the view to building their wealth.

4. People want to achieve their specific financial goals in life

5. People want to earn more than from a saving account.

6. People want to save for Retirement

7. People invest to save their Income Tax or to reduce their taxable income.

Tips on Investing

1. Invest Early. You lose the opportunity to build your wealth by keeping your money at home.

2. Reinvest income earned from your investments.

3. Invest at a good interest rate. The more income you earn which can then be reinvested.

4. You should invest at least 20% of your monthly income.

Three types of investment can grow your wealth

1. In Equity Shares or Mutual Funds. If dividend income is more than the interest rate.

2. In Gold. Not in Jewellery. You wouldn't get the correct value at the time of sale. It is better to invest in Gold Bonds.

3. In Real Estate. If the rental income you receive is more than 8% of the Return on investment.

Be Aware of Risks

Remember, investing is all about growing your money to achieve your goals, but you must invest cautiously.

Before investing, you must understand that different investment choices have different risks.

As a general rule, investments with high returns tend to be riskier. Therefore, the appropriate for you depends on how much risk you are prepared to take. Diversify your investment. Don't put all your eggs in one basket. Put your money into a variety of investments to minimize your risks of investing.

There are so many ways to generate your wealth through the right investments:

Safe Investments of Less Risk with Less Return

1.Term Deposit into Bank

2.Public Provident Fund (PPF) / National Pension Scheme (NPS)

3.Govt. Saving Schemes

4.Savings Bonds

5.Life Insurance

6.Real Estate

Unsafe Investment of Higher Risk with Higher Return

1. Mutual Funds

2. Shares / Stock Market

A few tips from experts in the capital market

Two very important lessons for those who want to invest in the stock market

(Time and patience, are two sides of the same coin)

***The value of patience**

***Short-term changes in stock prices may have little to do with the value**

UPSTOX is a right platform for the purchase of Equity Shares. Except for PAN Cards, no paperwork is required to invest in shares. Even though you can save so much of the charges which normally banks are charged.

Buffett. His success lies in his patient attitude. In this high-paced world of constant activity, Buffett purposefully operates at a slower speed. And by this process, Buffett and Berkshire are accumulating mountains of wealth. **Wealth creation reinvests into more cash-generating opportunities.**

Slow and steady always wins the race.

> **Have patience it takes to time to get to the success line.**

> **Focus on making $1 first, then focus on $10, Then $100, $1000, $10000, and so on.**

> **DON'T GET CAUGHT UP IN THE LONG TERM WHEN THE SHORT-TERM NEEDS FOCUS FIRST.**

If you want to invest in the share market

1. Save at least 20% of your income for investment

2. Invest your money in safe-investments

3. For investment in the share market, you require only a small amount

Investment in the share market

*You must know how to read the financial statement of a company. There are three financial statements.

1. Income Statement (Profit & Loss Account)

2. Balance Sheet

3. Cash Flow Statement

Purchase the stock when it trades below its intrinsic value even though the overall market is not substantially cheap. (When the Assets value of a company is more than the Market Value of the company)

Suppose the shares are sold for Rs 0.90 paise each, the market value of the company will be Rs.9 lac whereas its assets are for 10 lac (900000 / 1000000). This is the right time to purchase this company or its shares **when it trades below its intrinsic value even though the overall market is not substantially cheap. This is known as the principle of the Margin of Safety.**

If we cannot purchase the company for 9 lac then we can even purchase its shares. In this way we have saved our principal amount otherwise our formula of compounding would not work.

Each and every time we have to analyze the financial statements of the company before we invest in shares.

There are four important things to learn before investing in shares

1. **Bonds are safer than stock (shares)**

2. **Liquidity of assets should be in excess of the liabilities**

3. **Shares are purchased when the price of a share is below its intrinsic value in the market.**

4. **Sometimes companies show their Intangible Assets in the Balance sheet to increase the value of the company.**

FORMULA for Safe Investing in Share Market

Don't go for the news

Don't go for Tips from friends

Whereas the right formula is "Trend is your friend."

To know the right Price Trend of the shares of a particular company you can check it from the Technical Analysis of the websites of investing.com, moneycontrol.com

- On uptrend: You can purchase the shares

- On downtrend: You can sell the shares

- On sideways trend: You can wait to purchase or to sell and

Buffett is often asked what types of companies he will purchase in the future. One that possesses good economics and is run by trustworthy managers. He suggests to invest in:

*Insurance Companies

*Broadcasting companies, Newspapers, TV. (Broadcasting companies produce above-average returns on capital and generate substantial cash in excess of their operating needs)

*Network business, * Banking

* Information technology service (considered to be a growth defensive industry)

Chapter Six
Income Maximization Methods

How the Rich minimize their tax burden

There are few options for salaried persons to minimize their tax burden. And there are also limited exemptions available to individuals by the Govt. to minimize their tax burden. And they have to invest out of their saving (u/s 80C of Income Tax Act) to save the taxes which also reduce their cash flow from their pocket.

Whereas if they do any business (Profession, Partnership LLP or Company) then they have so many options to save their taxes by claiming expenses incurred to run the business i.e. why the rich get richer day by day.

Partnership Firm LLP

In the case of a person being a partner of a firm, which is separately assessed as such, the partner's share (Profit) in the total income of the firm is exempt from tax. The partnership firm is taxed as a separate entity. In computing the total income of the firm, any salary, bonus, commission, or remuneration paid to a partner, shall be deductible. The share of the partner in the total income of the firm will be fully exempt from income tax. In case of loss, the liability of partners is limited in LLP Firms.

Company

A company is a voluntary association of persons formed for the purpose of some business for profit with capital, divisible into shares, having a separate legal entity, and a common seal. A company can own property in its own name, have a bank account, owe money, or lend money to persons; it is an artificial juristic person with perpetual succession. Companies are mainly of two types…private limited and public limited.

The profit is distributed in the form of dividends which were also exempted from Income Tax but now it is taxable.

The dividend received from an Indian company was **exempt until 31 March 2020 (FY 2019-20)**

That was because the company declaring such a dividend already paid dividend distribution tax (DDT) before making payment.

However, the Finance Act, of 2020 changed the method of dividend taxation. Henceforth, all dividend received on or after 1 April 2020 is taxable in the hands of the investor/shareholder.

All companies, whether domestic or foreign, are liable to pay tax, irrespective of their income.

Depreciation: Business houses invest their capital in purchasing Assets. They claim depreciation as an expense in their business. This is the benefit given by Govt. to save taxes and to generate cash flow.

Most of the assets acquired by the business have some estimated period of service life and with the passage of time they lose in value due to any of the following reasons:

1.Through the wear and tear

2. With the passage of time (age)

3. An asset may not be able to meet the growing demand of a business

Thus, depreciation is a permanent, gradual, and continuing reduction in the book value of any fixed assets (with the exception of land).

Every depreciating asset needs to be replaced at the end of its useful life, which requires the withdrawal of substantial funds from the business. Thus, in order to run the business smoothly, sufficient funds are generated internally. Each year a part of the profits provided is for the replacement of the asset and it is known as depreciation.

There are several methods of charging depreciation annually. These are:

1. Straight Line Method:

Amount written off from year to year as depreciation is uniform.

At the end of its estimated life, only the scrap value of an asset remains in the books of accounts.

2. Written Down Value Method:

The rate of depreciation is uniform. This rate is applied to the cost of the asset as reduced by depreciation for earlier years. The amount of depreciation charge keeps on reducing every year.

The amount of yearly depreciation is treated as the expenses deducted from the total income of the business. The income tax is charged on the net income (after deducting the depreciation)

How we save tax through Depreciation

Example: Cars purchased for business   Rs. 50,00.000

      Less: Depreciation @ 15%   Rs. 7,50,000

      Our Profit is   Rs. 20,00,000

      Less: Depreciation   Rs. 7,50,000

      Net Profit   Rs. 12,50,000

Income Tax will be charged on Rs. 12,50,000, not on Rs.20,00,000

If the Rate of tax is 30% on Rs.20,00,000 it will be Rs.6,00,000

On Rs.12,50,000 it will be Rs.3,75,000

Income Tax Saved Rs.2,25,000

And expenses claimed Rs.7,50,000

This is the main saving in the business whereas an individual can't claim it and can't take the benefit of depreciation.

"Difficult roads often lead to beautiful destinations."

Chapter Seven
Financial Planning

Plan your financial investments in such a way that after retirement live a respectable life and that you do not feel a shortage of funds due to retirement and after you, your wife and children should live a respectable life.

Mutual Fund: It's a safe way to invest in the stock and debt market however who knows "what will be the rate of return after a period of three months"? Because they advertise that the MF has earned a certain amount in the three years. They hide each and every piece of information from investors and try to attract a high return in the future.

Investment in Gold: It is a good investment if it will be made in Gold Bonds. But if you invest in jewelry, a few problems you have to face:

*Price of Gold is not stable all the time

*Storage is risky

*Not easily sold

*It is dead money in the form of ornaments

Investment in Land:

*Requires lots of funds

*It is difficult to secure

*Ideal land always creates problems

*There are so many legal aspects

*Difficult to sell when the money is required

Purchase of House or Flat:

*Purchase of a big house with big problems. The building is not in your control.

*Difficult to maintain

*Maintenance charges are a liability even if it is vacant

*Property tax to pay

*If given on Rent then problems can be raised by tenants

*Burden of loan Interest and EMI

* Difficult to sell when the money is required

Life Insurance Policy:

*It is secure even if the rate of earning is low because it secures risk in life.

*LIC is a Govt. undertaking

*Their funds and assets make it more secure

*Loan can be taken at any time

*Any time it can be surrendered

*No legal formalities

*Lifelong a fixed return is possible.

*LIC is a lifetime guarantee

*Helpful in case of sudden death

*Can be helpful to create wealth without any risk

BANK

*When closed you can't get your own money

*Rate of interest is not certain, changes and reduces year by year

* Bank loan is a trap you cannot control even in the future people had to leave their property with the bank for non-payment whereas in LIC. The investment is under your control even if you did not pay but you will receive a Bonus year by year

Inflation is a Silent Killer, make sure you invest your money to beat inflation, otherwise, it's going to be worthless.

RULES OF MONEY: GIVE EVERY DOLLAR A JOB

RECAP

HOW TO INVEST?

Top Reasons to Invest
- Protect Your Purchasing Power.
- Grow Your Capital.
- Achieve Your Financial Goals.
- Earn More Than Earn a Savings Account.
- Diversify Your Income.
- Save for Retirement.
- Lower Taxable Income.

Investing is not a choice in the normal sense but a matter of habit. The ideal first habit to form is to start investing a small regular amount through Recurring deposits or SIP.

Compound interest means you not only earn returns on the principal money that you invest but also get to enjoy a return on the interest income that keeps adding to your principal. This process continues until you withdraw your money. In simple terms, with compound interest, you can grow your wealth by just staying put in your investments.

Successful small businesses are often built on the pursuit of a personal hobby or interest. Most important merge your passion and skill with something that is useful to other people.

The goal of business is profit. There's nothing wrong with having a hobby, but if you want to call it a business, you have to make money. There are two important things to understand.

1.   **Spend as little money as possible to start your project**

2.   **Make as much money as you can.**

Your success in business depends upon three principles:

1.Product or service: what you sell

2.People willing to pay for it

3. Sell What People Buy

Nothing will change your life faster than building new skills. Dedicate time during your day to build your skills. Learn them via business books, and videos but don't forget to physically practice your skills too.

You should know your weaknesses and strength. If you are influenced by the opinions of others, you will have no DESIRE of your own. You have a brain and mind of your own. Use it and reach your own decisions.

Three types of investment can grow your wealth

*In Equity Shares or Mutual Funds. If dividend income is more than the interest rate.

* In Gold. Not in Jewellery. You wouldn't get the correct value at the time of sale. It is better to invest in Gold Bonds.

* In Real Estate. If the rental income you receive is more than 8% of the Return on investment.

A few tips from experts in the capital market

> **Two very important lessons for those who want to invest in the stock market**

(Time and patience, are two sides of the same coin)

***The value of patience**

***Short-term changes in stock prices may have little to do with the value.**

If you want to invest in the share market

1. Save at least 20% of your income for investment
2. Invest your money in safe- investments
3. For investment in the share market, you required only a small amount

Purchase the stock when it trades below its intrinsic value even though the overall market is not substantially cheap. (When the Assets value of a company is more than the Market Value of the company)

FORMULA for Safe Investing in Share Market

Don't go for the news

Don't go for Tips from friends

Whereas the right formula is "Trend is your friend."

There are few options for salaried persons to minimize their tax burden. And there are also limited exemptions available to individuals by the Govt. to minimize their tax burden.

The partnership firm is taxed as a separate entity. In computing the total income of the firm, any salary, bonus, commission, or remuneration paid to a partner, shall be deductible. The share of the partner in the total income of the firm will be fully exempt from income tax. In case of loss, the liability of partners is limited in LLP Firms.

Depreciation: Business houses invest their capital in purchasing Assets. They claim depreciation as an expense in their business. This is the benefit given by Govt. to save taxes and to generate cash flow. **This is the main saving in the business whereas an individual can't claim it and can't take the benefit of depreciation.**

Plan your financial investments in such a way that after retirement live a respectable life and that you do not feel a shortage of funds due to retirement and after you, your wife and children should live a respectable life.

Stage-4
Multiply Money (How to Create Wealth)

Warren Buffet said….

You can't physically work 24/7, But your money can. If you don't find a way to make money while you sleep, you will work until you die.

You attract what you think about whatever you are thinking about, you are attracting.

If you want to attract more money, start thinking about your finances, how you are going to make more money, and how you are going to save.

Making money is an Action

Keeping money is behaviour

Growing money is knowledge

Wealth is not about money, it is a mindset.

Instant wins, won't make you wealthy, but your actions will

Chapter One
Effects of Compounding

Your monthly investment of Rs.1000 can be Rs. 1.43 Crore after 30 years

Your monthly investment of Rs.500 can be Rs.71.62 Lac after 30 years

This is the Magic of Compounding.

Compounding is the process in which an asset's earnings, from either capital or interest, are reinvested to generate additional earnings over time. This growth, calculated using exponential functions, occurs because the investment will generate earnings from both its initial principal and the accumulated earnings from preceding periods.

Compounding, therefore, differs from linear growth, where only the principal earns interest each period.

KEY TAKEAWAYS

- Compounding is the process whereby interest is credited to an existing principal amount as well as to interest already paid.

- Compounding thus can be construed as interest on interest—the effect of which is to magnify returns to interest over time, the so-called "miracle of compounding."

Compounding typically refers to the increasing value of an asset due to the interest earned on both a principal and accumulated interest. This phenomenon, which is a direct realization of the time value of money (TMV) concept, is also known as compound interest.

Increased Compounding Periods

The effects of compounding strengthen as the frequency of compounding increases. Assume a one-year time period. The more compounding periods throughout this one year, the higher the future value of the investment, so naturally, two compounding periods per year are better than one, and four compounding periods per year are better than two.

To illustrate this effect, consider the following example given in the above formula. Assume that an investment of $1 million earns 20% per year. The resulting future value, based on a varying number of compounding periods, is:

- **Annual compounding (n = 1):** FV = $1,000,000 $\times [1 + (20\%/1)]^{(1 \times 1)}$ = $1,200,000

- **Semi-annual compounding (n = 2):** FV = $1,000,000 $\times [1 + (20\%/2)]^{(2 \times 1)}$ = $1,210,000

- **Quarterly compounding (n = 4):** FV = $1,000,000 $\times [1 + (20\%/4)]^{(4 \times 1)}$ = $1,215,506

- **Monthly compounding (n = 12):** FV = $1,000,000 $\times [1 + (20\%/12)]^{(12 \times 1)}$ = $1,219,391

- **Weekly compounding (n = 52):** FV = $1,000,000 $\times [1 + (20\%/52)]^{(52 \times 1)}$ = $1,220,934

- **Daily compounding (n = 365):** FV = $1,000,000 $\times [1 + (20\%/365)]^{(365 \times 1)}$ = $1,221,336

- Example of Compounding
- To illustrate how compounding works, suppose $10,000 is held in an account that pays 5% interest annually. After the first year or compounding period, the total in the account has risen to $10,500, a simple reflection of $500 in interest being added to the $10,000 principal In year two, the account realizes a 5% growth on both the original principal and the $500 of first-year interest, resulting in a second-year gain of $525 and a balance of $11,025.

Example of Compounding

Compounding Period	Starting Balance	Interest	Ending Balance
1	$10,000.00	$500.00	$10,500.00
2	$10,500.00	$525.00	$11,025.00
3	$11,025.00	$551.25	$11,576.25
4	$11,576.25	$578.81	$12,155.06
5	$12,155.06	$607.75	$12,762.82
6	$12,762.82	$638.14	$13,400.96
7	$13,400.96	$670.05	$14,071.00
8	$14,071.00	$703.55	$14,774.55
9	$14,774.55	$738.73	$15,513.28
10	$15,513.28	$775.66	$16,288.95

- $10,000 Investment Earning 5% Compounded Interest
- After 10 years, assuming no withdrawals and a steady 5% interest rate, the account would grow to $16,288.95. Without having added or removed anything from our principal balance except for interest, the impact of compounding has increased the change in balance from $500 in Period 1 to $775.66 in Period 10.

- In addition, without having added new investment on our own, our investment has grown by $6,288.95 in 10 years. Had the investment only paid simple interest (5% on the original investment only), annual interest would have only been $5,000 ($500 per year for 10 years).

Compounding on Investments and Debt

- Compound interest works on both Assets and Liabilities. While compounding boosts the value of an asset more rapidly, it can also increase the amount of money owed on a loan, as interest accumulates on the unpaid principal and previous interest charges. Even if you make loan payments, compounding interest may result in the amount of money you owe is greater in future periods.

- The same compounding is used for payment of EMI on loans taken from any Bank

- Example:

- If we want a Housing Loan of Rs. 50 Lakh @ 9% Rate of Interest for 25 years

- We have to pay Rs.42000 pm as EMI and for total Interest, we have to pay Rs.76 Lakh

- Whereas if we invest Rs.4000 in monthly SIP of MF@ 13% for 25 years.

- We have to Invest a total of Rs.1200000 and will get a Return of Rs.7885740 and whereas the value of our Investment will be Rs.9085740 after a period of 25 years.

Effect of Compounding on EMI

Your EMI of 25 years can be reduced to 10 years. This all can be possible with a simple method of compounding.

1   If you increase your **EMI** from 12 in a year to 13, your EMI will come down to 20 years.

2   If you increase your **EMI** with 5%, it will come down to 13.5 years

3   If you increase your **EMI** with 10% ,it will come down to 10 years

The Rule of 72 is used to estimate how long an investment or savings will double in value if there is compound interest (or compounding returns). The rule states that the number of years it will take to double is 72 divided by the interest rate. If the interest rate is 5% with compounding, it would take around 14 years and five months to double

"Miracles start to happen when you give as much energy to your dreams as you do to your fears."

Chapter Two
Effect of Inflation

At present, the Inflation Rate is 7%, and the value of Rs. One Crore will be:

After 10 years Rs.50 Lakh

After 15 years Rs.36 Lakh

After 20 years Rs.25 Lakh

And for the Full Proof of Financial Planning, our rate of Return on our Investment should be higher than the Rate of Inflation.

At present, the Rate of Return on these Investments is Alarming for us.

Highest 3-Year FD Interest Rates

Name of Bank	For General Citizens (p.a.)	For Senior Citizens (p.a.)
Axis Bank	7%	7.75%
IDBI Bank	6.50%	7%
State Bank of India	6%	6.50%

Saving Account — 3 to 4%

Recurring Deposits — 5.80% to 6.20%

Post office Monthly Income Scheme — 7.40%

Post office Time Deposit — 6.80 to 7.50%

5year NSC	7.70%
Kisan Vikas Patra	7.50%
Public Provident Fund	7.10%
Senior Citizens Saving Scheme	8.20%
Sukanya Samriddhi Yojana	8%

We are just consuming our principal for investing in the above deposit schemes because the return on investment (except for 6 schemes) is even less than the rate of Inflation which is at present 7%.

The highest and quick returns are in the Share Market but it is not a safe investment

Then how can we earn more quickly and safely?.

The safest method is Mutual Fund SIP (Systematic Investment Plan). Here the team of experts manages our account. The current Rate of Return on MF SIP is 15% to 18%, but there may be a risk if the team who manages your sip is not much efficient.

The safest way is to start a SIP of MF in the Index Fund of Nifty Fifty only. The rate of return might be 1% low for MF, but it will be safe as the investment will be to the best 50 companies listed in the Index.

You can even check it online from Mutual Fund Calculator

Systematic Investment Plan Calculation (SIP of Rs.500 pm)

	1	2	3
Monthly Investment	Rs. 500	Rs. 500	Rs. 500
Expected Return Rate p.a	18%	18%	18%
Time Period	10	20	30
Investment Amount	60000	120000	180000
Estimated Return	108129	1051744	6982645
Total Value	168129	1171744	7162645

Systematic Investment Plan Calculation (SIP of Rs.1000 pm)

	1	2	3
Monthly Investment	Rs. 1000	Rs.1000	Rs. 1000
Expected Return Rate p.a	18%	18%	18%
Time Period	10	20	30
Investment Amount	120000	240000	360000
Estimated Return	216258	2103487	13965289
Total Value	336258	2343487	14325289

Systematic Investment Plan Calculation (SIP of Rs.5000 pm)

	1	2	3
Monthly Investment	Rs. 5000	Rs.5000	Rs. 5000
Expected Return Rate p.a	18%	18%	18%
Time Period	10	20	30
Investment Amount	600000	1200000	1800000
Estimated Return	1081288	10517436	69826446
Total Value	1681288	11717436	71626446

"Great opportunities are not seen with your eyes.
They are seen with your mind." -Robert Kiyosaki

Chapter- Three
Time is Money

We know money is precious. However, we usually ignore another precious resource, time, we should value time as much as we value money-wasting it is similar to wasting money.

How can you add one more month to your working- life?

Get up at 5 am instead of 7 am

You saved 2 hours daily

In a week you saved 14 hours

In a year 728 hours

728 hours is equal to one month

Some useful tips on how to utilise your time to the fullest to enhance your wealth.

.. Narendra Nathan.

1.Create a schedule

Just like a budget ensures money discipline, a calendar ensures time discipline.

* List all your task and assignments.

* Define priorities

* Estimate the time each task will take.

* Identify the time you want for leisure.

2.Don't kill time

Since time is a precious and finite resource. Use the extra time to learn a new skill and thus increase earnings potential.

3.Maximise savings when time allows

Expenses are low when one is single and is thus the best time to save money optimally. Invest in growth assets like equities for compounding at higher rates.

4.Use gadgets to save time

A significant amount of time can be saved by using home appliances. This will increase spending but you can use the saved time to earn more. Make sure that the saved time is used productively.

5.Consider the opportunity cost of time

We can save money by doing all the work ourselves, but it is not practical because we don't have the required time or expertise. Though this will increase expenses, the time saved can be used productively. Outsource work to experts.

6.Don't idle after retirement

Income from small work or satisfaction from social service will be in addition to reduced health costs. Retire from work but not from life.

7.Respect time schedules of others

You may end up losing money if you don't respect the time schedules of others. You may lose business if you keep your client waiting. Respecting other's time is a must if you want others to respect your time.

"One Year = 365 Opportunities
A wise man will make more opportunities than he finds.
Be a wise man."

Chapter Four
How to Make Your Dreams Come True?

"Dreams are the seeds of change. Nothing ever grows without a seed, and nothing ever changes without a dream."
—Debby Boone

When you find a dream inside your heart, don't ever let it go...

Because dreams are the tiny seeds, from which beautiful tomorrow grows.......III

It's never too late to reinvent yourself.

Start a whole new life at 70

Stop Saying you can't

You can and you should

Dreams don't have an expiration

The harder the Journey the Stronger you will Become.

A man without a dream is like a body without a soul.

Start seeing big dreams & you will automatically get the courage to pursue them.

When you truly want something and go after it without limiting your belief, the Universe will make it happen.

Dream of a Bike and Get it.

Dream of a Car and Get it.

Dream for a House and Get it.

Dream of Money and Earn it.

The most successful people start with a dream in mind —a dream of something fascinating and wonderful. You can rest assured that if you can dream it, you can do it.

Dream Big

Think Big

Trust yourself and

Make it Happen

You can make your dreams come true if you have the right mindset, put in the right effort, and make a reasonable plan. There are Five steps to achieving your dreams.

1.Note Down the Big Dreams (Idea without Action is Nothing)

You must know exactly what you want. Being specific about your goals and dreams will help you achieve them faster. One way to be very specific about it and keep it in your mind is to write it in a diary. If you don't know what you're looking for, you won't be able to achieve it.

2. Time Bound Your Dreams (Hunt your Goal like a Hungry Beast)

Setting Deadlines have magical powers. Things are in their tracks and are getting things done.

3.Create a Plan of Action for a Specific Goal (Dreams become reality when thoughts become Actions)

"Words can inspire thoughts can provoke, but only action truly brings you closer to your Dreams".   If you want to purchase a car. And its price is Rs.10 Lakh, you want it within a period of 3years. To make your dream true you have to save Rs.27778 per month (Rs.28000/-pm). Daily you have to save Rs.950/-

4. Goal Should be Achievable If you want to go to Agra by your Bike. Agra is 200 km. the speed of your Bike is 50 Km per hour. Then you can reach Agra in 4 hours. If you fix your Goal to reach Agra in three hours then with the speed of 50Km per hour, it can not be possible. Your Goal should be achievable otherwise you would not be able to achieve it. And on the other hand, if you save Rs.10000 per month instead of Rs.28000 then how can you achieve your goal in 3 years to purchase the car of your dream?

5. Be Consistence in your Plan Once the fog lifts and your road map starts to become clear. You have got to put in the work to achieve your goals. You can become true if you are:

i).**Persistent** If you want to achieve your dreams, you must know that in the process, not everything will go as you have planned. You can't get negative and pessimist because of some failures along the way. Even if something goes wrong, stay positive, and maintain your confidence.

ii).**Efforts** You can make your dreams come true if you have the right mindset, put in the right effort, and make a reasonable plan. There will be some ups and downs along the way, but if you learn from your downfalls, you'll be more likely to reach your dreams,

iii).Motivation: Visualizing success can help you manifest it. Close your eyes and picture how you'd feel once your goal is accomplished. This is a great motivational technique of achieving your goals.

Hard Work + Dreams + Dedication = Success

"Do not store your dreams in your eyes, they may roll down with tears.
Store them in your heart each heartbeat will inspire you to fullfill them."

Chapter Five
Stay Dedicated, it Doesn't Happen Overnight

The growth of wealth depends on three main points

1.Persistent: Continue doing something even though people say that you are wrong or that you cannot do it.

2.Consistency: Consistency is the critical driver for success. Being consistent means dedicating yourself to your goals and staying focused on the things and activities to achieve your goals.

3.Discipline: Discipline leads to Habits, Habits lead to consistency, and Consistency leads to Growth.

We can even create a large wealth through investment in Life Insurance if we planned to invest in a calculated way

(1) A Young man of 25 years if he invests monthly Rs.26872 for 25 years in the combination of three Plans, he will get:

1. Rs.69 Lakh.   after completion of the 25th year,

2. Family Risk Cover: 1 crore to 3.23 crores

3. Accident Risk Cover: 2 crores to 3 crores

4. Wealth created: 6 crores

(2) A Young man can get a Return @ 13% Per Annam for a Lifetime with a combination of two plans for investing Rs.10 Lakh

(3) At a time when the inflation has reached 7% even then, you can earn a lifetime pension @ 8% by investing for a period of time in the LIC.

(4) **LIC PLANS CAN BE CUSTOMISED AS PER REQUIREMENTS.**

Suppose a person wants to purchase a LIC Policy, but has different requirements, and wants no maturity amount. A LIC Plan can be prepared on a settlement basis to maintain the same lifestyle after retirement.

There is no maturity amount. The insured will get Rs.847583 every year from age 65 to 79.

The Premium payment term is for 10 years from age 49 to 58.

The total payment in 10 years is Rs.5063849 (Rs.505273 per year)

Amount of total Return will come to 151%

Rs.12713745 (Rs 847583 yearly from age 65 to 79)

"Rome wasn't built in a day, but they were laying bricks every day.

You don't have build everything you want today, just lay a brick."

RECAP

Compounding is the process in which an asset's earnings, from either capital or interest, are reinvested to generate additional earnings over time.

Compounding thus can be construed as interest on interest—the effect of which is to magnify returns to interest over time, the so-called "miracle of compounding."

And for the Full Proof of Financial Planning, our rate of Return on our Investment should be higher than the Rate of Inflation.

The safest way is to start a SIP of MF in the Index Fund of Nifty Fifty only. The rate of return might be 1% low for MF, but it will be safe as the investment will be to the best 50 companies listed in the Index.

We know money is precious. However, we usually ignore another precious resource, time, we should value time as much as we value money-wasting it is similar to wasting money.

A man without a dream is like a body without a soul.

Start seeing big dreams & you will automatically get the courage to pursue them.

When you truly want something and go after it without limiting your belief, the Universe will make it happen.

You can make your dreams come true if you have the right mindset, put in the right effort, and make a reasonable plan.

The growth of wealth depends on three main points

1.Persistent: Continue doing something even though people say that you are wrong or that you cannot do it.

2.Consistency: Consistency is the critical driver for success. Being consistent means dedicating yourself to your goals and staying focused on the things and activities to achieve your goals.

3.Discipline: Discipline leads to Habits, Habits lead to consistency, and Consistency leads to Growth.

We can even create a large wealth through investment in Life Insurance, if we planned to invest in a calculated way.

Stage-5
How to Maintain Wealth

Earning is not much difficult as compared to maintaining the earned wealth. We normally see lottery winner always lose their money because they do not have that much financial knowledge to save and invest in a proper way.

A lesson about Money. If you can't manage $1000 then you can't manage $10000.

You do not suddenly learn how to handle money by amassing more of it. This is why a lot of Lottery winners lose it all.

How you can have a check on your money spending

Tips for Money Management

1. **Keep track of your spending.** If you know where your money is going it will be easier to make changes if you need to.

2. **Separate wants from needs.** Do you really need that 42-inch flat-screen television? When money is tight it should not be spent unless absolutely necessary.

3. **Avoid using credit to pay your bills.** While it may make things easier now, using credit only increases your monthly payments in the future.

4. **Save regularly.** Have some of your pay cheque directly deposited into your savings account

5. **Cut or downgrade your services.** Can you get a cheaper cable package or have no cable at all? If you have a cell phone consider cutting your landline.

6. **Try lowering your energy bill.** Turn off appliances and lights when they are not needed. Purchase energy-efficient lightbulbs. When you can, use a fan instead of air conditioning or put on a sweater instead of turning on the heater.

7. **Cut down on take-out ordering.** Even if the meal is not expensive, doing it frequently can really add up.

"Sometimes the smallest step in the right direction ends up being the biggest step in your life."

Chapter One
Golden Rule to Success

Let us know the Golden Rule to Success:

1.Pay yourself First

2.Save at least 20% of your Income

3.Have an Emergency Fund

4.Put your Money to Work

FIRST PURCHASE ASSETS (Property) Than COMFORT

One case study of my assistant:

**"If you truly want to change your life,
You must be first willing to change your mind."**

I was a tax consultant cum internal auditor in a company and used to visit twice a week. The owner of that company was not honest and was not a good paymaster. He recruited employees of the lower middle class so that he had to pay them even less than the minimum fixed wages. One of his accountants was very hard working but his salary was very low. It was not possible for him to meet his expenses. Once I caught him with fraud of a small amount of Rs.20000/- in the year 1980. He requested me not disclose it to the owner.

I told him that I will deduct a small amount from his salary every month and would not tell him about the fraud but he has to promise me that he would invest that amount in a property so that the amount could be utilized for benefit of his family.

He purchased a small plot to construct his house with that amount in a very cheap colony. Later I left that assignment because I was not satisfied with the behavior of that owner. After a period of 25 years once I met that accountant in another company. He was there in a good position and was earning a good salary. He was thankful to me for my guidance which I had suggested to him, to invest in the property. He told me that from the amount received on the sale of the same plot he had purchased a house for his family and the balance amount he deposited into a bank to earn good interest and which will be used at the time of his daughter's marriage.

If I had not suggested him to purchase the Property, then he might have used it for his household expenses or in any other way. The right time planning gave him a good result.

PAY YOURSELF FIRST (Save 20% from your Income Regularly)

"Take care of yourself first or you will have nothing left to give others.

Self-care is not selfishness. You cannot serve from an empty vessel."

Everyone has the ambition to grow rich, but I always suggest to my assistants that whatever you do to earn an extra income you should pay first to yourself for your expenses and if there are any savings left then you should invest it with proper planning and without proper market research should not think to start any business.

One of my assistants was over-ambitious and wanted to be rich overnight. Without my knowledge, he took a shop on rent to start a business for his wife, of ladies' garments. He wanted his wife to earn something and contribute to his income. But even in a small business, you cannot start without proper planning. Now all the burden of the shop was on his shoulder. And he had to leave his job.

Due to the loss of salary income, he had to take a loan from friends but as per the commitment to return in time, he had to increase the burden on his credit cards. The loan amount increased so much that he was not in a position to pay even the interest of the loan. He had to close his shop and again went searching for a job. But He was so frustrated that he was not in a position to take up a job.

OUTSOURCE (Save your time to learn more and outsource your work)

"While building your team, always search for people who love to win.

If it is difficult to find, at least look for people who hate to lose."

I was appointed as an internal auditor in a Tata dealership, and it was a part of my duty to go to their branches in Bihar. The employees of the branch office were very much cordial to me because I taught many things related to accounts and taxation which no one was interested to teach them. I believe in teamwork, this way my labour of work was reduced, and I could utilise my skill in the improvement and development of the company in which I was working as an Accounts Head.

IMPROVE YOUR SKILLS

"People who have overcome darkness in their life typically have a fire inside them that is almost impossible to extinguish." (Stephen Timoney)

I used to visit an NGO twice a week for accounts and taxation purposes. This NGO was for the uplifting of women from poor classes. They provided job oriental training on a nominal- charge so that one could earn to meet one's household expenses after getting training from that institution.

Once when I was sitting in the account's office one lady around 30 years looking very helpless came to the office- in-charge and wanted to enquire regarding any job for her. She was in dire need of a job and her eyes were filled with tears. But the officer simply refused to her. I was listening to her story that her husband is ill for the last so many years, and she has been treated as a servant in her in-law's house and has to beg for food. She was about to leave but I asked her to wait for a minute.

As I came to know that her education was only 10th standard, but she wanted to do any type of work in the office. She was intelligent and wanted to learn to get the job. I suggested she join Computer and English classes so that her working skill could improve. But she was not in a position to pay the fee for Computer and English classes. I requested the Chairperson to exempt her fee or if they want, I promised to pay on her behalf with a request that it should not be disclosed to her. She was very much thankful to the Chairperson and started the next day to learn the computer.

It was by chance that the officer in charge had to go on a long leave. I had confidence in her and suggested the Chairperson give her work related to the administration of the office and I had confidence that she will manage and, wherever required, I was ready to help her. Within a very short period of time, she came to know all the official work and the Chairperson was also pleased with her work. It was amazing that she picked up the work very quickly. If anyone has an interest and willpower to learn then all are there to help that person. After a long leave, the officer in charge came and joined her duty, and she was surprised to see her working confidently.

She has learned to keep the official documents and many more official- work. I came to know that she was in search of a job. She has improved her skill and has the confidence to do any work. I referred her to a company known to me and they appointed her to maintain official records and to attend their phone calls. Once she called me and thanked me for creating such confidence in her to make her capable to earn her living. I know when any person has a very strong desire to improve his/her skill, then no one can stop success from coming his/her way.

THINK WIN-WIN (Learn to Win)

"The people who get on in this world are the people who get up and look for the circumstances they want and, if they can't find them, make them." (George Bernard Shaw)

I was watching a great finale of "Big Boss" on TV. Everyone was interested to know who is going to win the final prize of Rs. 50 lac. There were five finalists in the final round. Only one has to win the prize. We all were very anxious to know the name of the final winner. Before announcing the name of the winner, they gave an option to all of the finalists that anyone out of the five has a choice to exit from this contest and can take Rs. 10 lac with him. No one wanted to exit. But we were surprised to see one out of these five took Rs.10 lac and made his exit from the competition. This is the attitude to win. He knows that if he does not win then he would not get anything. This is the right time to change his failure to succeed.

People with a positive attitude are optimistic. They focus on "can" instead of "can't."

They are always in the right place at the right time. People who create their own luck are mentally, physically, and emotionally ready to perform at their maximum. They arc learners and hard workers. Thcy developed their skills over time and earned the right to capitalize on their opportunities. They don't complain or curse their bad luck, they just make a change. In addition, they are extremely open and able to take advantage of new opportunities that may arise as they pursue their original goal.

"Our eyes are placed in front because it is more important to look ahead than to look back."

Keep this in mind for your success in life.

1. You are continuously learning and applying.

2. You don't let other people's opinions affect your mental peace and life

3. You don't run away from difficult situations rather you face them and try to get out of them.

4. You are kind and humble and always ready to help the needy

5. You know the value of time and don't let it go wasted

6. You always get up whenever you have a setback in your life.

Chapter-Two
Create Assets for Lifetime

You should create these earned assets in your lifetime to earn income

1. **Business**: Your own business can help you to earn more and can give you freedom of time. Once you establish your business It will give lifetime income. Secrets of a Successful Businessman

    *Low Margin and High number of Customers

    *Sweet voice and Respect to customers

    *Receive less but no credit

    *Low Margin to retain customers for long times

    *Full use of money value, no misuse of money

    *Wide Net Work

    *Treat Staff as Family

    *Negotiation Skills for Purchases

    *Learn how to earn without your own investments

2. **Real Estate / Land**: Land is limited and demand for land is increasing day by day. Once you purchase it will pay you a long time. The land you can sell at any time and its value will enhance during the duration of time.

3. **Stock (Paper assets)**: Investment in equity shares. There is no limit to earning if you have proper knowledge of the share market. Treat it as a long-term investment to earn more.

4. **Gold / Silver**: One must invest in Gold & Silver. This investment is essential for your emergency. Investment in ornaments is not a good investment. You have to invest in Gold Bonds.

5. **Cash in hand (power in your hand)**: Cash itself is power. You must have the cash to meet your three months' expenses. Having Cash is an easy process to purchase anything at any time.

6. **Equipment & Accessories**: If you use your equipment to earn income out of its Rent then it is a good source of income. Rent on Generator, Computers and car, etc

7. **Copyright, Trademark, and Patents**: If you are a writer then you can create a copyright on your books, Singer can have a copyright on their songs, and an Artist can have a copyright on their paintings. If you have established your business and you want to register your company's name so that no one can take advantage of the hard work which you utilised to establish your business then you have to register your company's trade- mark, Patent & logo.

8. **Brand name**: It's your goodwill to establish your Brand name. When a brand name is added to a product then its sale value can be even 10 times more than its actual value.

9. **Network**: The collection of customer data is the main source of network marketing. The return is more or even multiplied if your network is strong.

10. Website: Today your website plays an important role to increase your business. In today's time, your marketing is not limited to your local area. It has a wide reach to the whole world.

Free Assets should develop to increase your value (Personal Wealth for a lifetime)

1. Time. Time is limited. Invest on you
2. Family and Friends
3. Skill
4. Knowledge
5. Mindset
6. Our body / Our health
7. Personal Brand
8. Your Channel on social sites
9. Your Skill / Passion based business
10. Your Resources
11. Creativity

"In the end, we only regret the chances we didn't take."

Chapter-Three
How Much Cash or Gold Can You Have With You?

Without any fear from ED (Enforcement Directorate), Income Tax Act (CBDT), Custom & Excise Act, and FEMA (Foreign Exchange Management Act)

1.Restrictions on Cash Transactions

Payment or aggregate of payment to any person on a single day in respect of purchases or any expenditure exceeding Rs.10000 (Rs.35000 in case of payment for plying, hiring, or leasing goods carriages)

2.Restriction on Acceptance of Loans, Deposits, etc of Rs.20000 or more in Cash.

No person can take a loan or accept a deposit or a sum, as advance or otherwise, in relation to the transfer of immovable property, of Rs.20000 or more from any other person, except by an account payee cheque/draft or by using an electronic clearing system.

3. Restriction on Receipt of Rs.2 lakh or more in Cash.

No person shall receive an amount of Rs. 200000 or more-

(i)   In aggregate from a person in a day, or

(ii)   In respect of a single transaction, or

(iii) In respect of transactions relating to one event or occasion from a person.

4. Restriction on Cash Donations

Donations to specified charitable Institutions (u/s 80G) of Income Tax Act. exceeding Rs.2000 shall not be deductible if it is paid in Cash.

Donations to political parties (u/s 80GGB and 80GGC) of Incom Tax Act irrespective of the amount shall be not deductible if it is paid in cash.

How much cash you can have with you?

You can have as much cash with you in your home or in your business provided:

1. You can prove the source of cash with you.

2. You have proof to show why you are having that much cash with you and it is properly accounted for if it is related to business.

3. If you do not have valid proof for holding cash over its limits, then you may have to pay a 137% of penalty on the total unaccounted cash with you.

4. Any *person can carry Rs.*250000 without any type of documents, if a *person carries* more than Rs.2.5 Lakhs then he/she must *carry* any proof or have to prove the source.

5. There is a limit of Rs. 25,000 per person for Indian residents to carry from India to the US.

6. Any person residing outside India may take outside India currency notes of the Government of India and Reserve Bank of India notes up to an amount not exceeding Rs.25,000 (Rupees Twenty- Five Thousand only) per person

7. Residents of India are allowed to carry up to Rs. 25,000 though. There's no limit, however, to how much foreign currency you can bring into India. Although, you will have to declare it if the amount exceeds US$ 5,000 in notes and coins, or US$10,000 in notes, coins, and traveler's cheques.

How much Gold you can have with you?

No maximum limit to holding Gold

If you have acquired the gold from explained sources of income including inheritance then there is **no maximum limit** on holding of gold jewellery or ornaments. However, your ITR should correspond to the amount of gold that you are holding.

Moreover, it is advised that you keep the invoice for your purchase. In case of an exchange of gold jewellery, keep a copy of the invoice of the exchange along with the invoice of the original purchase.

In case of inheritance, it is advised to keep a copy of the Will. It acts as proof of your inheritance. If the person from whom you have inherited the gold was a wealthy taxpayer it becomes easier to establish the quantity of gold inherited by you.

Wealth tax has been abolished but you still have a liability to disclose your wealth in case it exceeded Rs 30 lacs and file the return up to 31 March 2015. So if you have filed your wealth tax return where you have disclosed the gold you own then your ownership gets verified and you can keep the gold.

What if you can't explain the source of your gold?

The circular issued by CBDT specifies that a married lady is allowed to keep up to 500 grams of gold jewellery; an unmarried lady can hold up to 250 grams and a male member of the family can keep up to 100 grams of gold ornaments and jewelry.

Under the above-specified limit, it includes both inherited and purchased gold jewellery. Even if you don't have supporting documents for the above amount of gold jewelry, it will not be seized. However, it **does not include gold coins and bars.** The gold coins and bars can be seized even if it is within the limit specified above.

Chapter-Four
How to Influence the Customers

The book "INFLUENCE" was written by Robert B. Cialdini
In this book, the writer has explained in detail the "Weapons to Influence the customers.

1. **Price alone has a quality to attract.**

    Price alone had become a principal feather for quality. "Expensive= is considered as Good"

    Since normally the price of an item increases along with its worth: a higher price typically reflects the higher quality of the product and attracts rich customers. It is generally known that the costly products are good in quality which is why to attract the HNIs (High net-worth Individuals) customers the price of the products is fixed as on the higher side.

2. **Principle of Contrast**

    There is a principle the contrast, that affects the way we see the difference between two things that are presented one after another. Retail clothiers are a good example. Clothing stores instruct their sales personnel to sell the costly item first. Common sense might suggest the reverse: If a man has just spent a lot of money to purchase the first item, he may be reluctant to spend very much more on the purchase of a second item. They behave in accordance with what the contrast principle would suggest: Sell the suit first because when it comes time to look at sweaters, even expensive ones, their prices will not seem as high in comparison.

3. **Reciprocation:**

The rule says that we should try to repay, in kind, what another person has provided us. If a man does us a favour, we should do him one in return. If a man sends us a birthday present, we should remember his birthday with a gift of our own: if a couple invites us to a party, we should be sure to invite them to one of ours.

The Hare Krishna Group are very brilliant. They switched to a fund-raising tactic that made it unnecessary for target persons to have positive feelings toward the fund-raisers. They began to employ a donation-request procedure that engaged the rule for reciprocation. Before a donation is requested, the target person is given a "gift" –a book (Bhagavad Gita) or in the most cost-effective version, a flower. The unsuspecting passer-by who suddenly finds a flower pressed into his hands or pinned to his jacket is under no circumstances allowed to give it back, even if he asserts that he does not want it. A favourite place for free samples is the supermarket, where customers are frequently provided with small cubes of a certain variety of Biscuits or eatables to try.

By virtue of the reciprocity rule, then, we are obligated to the future repayment of favours, gifts, invitations, and the like.

4. The Rule Enforces Uninvited Debts

We should provide others with the kind of actions they have provided us: it does not require us to have asked for what we have received in order to feel obligated to repay.

There is an obligation to give, an obligation to receive, and an obligation to repay."

Some stores offer Coke to their customers and the ability of uninvited gifts to produce feelings of obligation is recognized by a variety of organizations. Even something as small as the price of a drink can produce a feeling of debt.

A small initial favour can produce a sense of obligation to agree to a substantially large return favour.

5. Commitment is the Key

Once a commitment is taken, there is a natural tendency to behave in ways that are stubbornly consistent with the stand.

Yet another reason, that written commitments are so effective is that they require more work than verbal ones. And the evidence is clear that the more effort that goes into a commitment, the greater its ability to influence the attitudes of the person who made it.

6. **Social Proof**

**Where all think alike, no one thinks very much. —
Walter Lippmann**

The principle of social proof says so: The greater the
number of people who find any idea correct, the more the
idea will be correct.

 Usually, when a lot of people are doing something, it is
the right thing to do. This feature of the principle of social
proof is simultaneously its major strength and its major
weakness.

Advertisers love to inform us when a product is the
"fastest-growing" or "largest-selling" because they don't
have to convince us directly that the product is good, they
need only say that many others think so, which seems
proof enough.

Salesmen are taught to spice their pitches with numerous
accounts of individuals who have purchased the product.

The principle of social proof operates most powerfully
when we are observing the behaviour of people just like
us. Therefore, we are more inclined to follow the lead of
a similar individual than a dissimilar one.

The second source of social evidence came from the
reactions of the crowd itself. We seem to assume that if a
lot of people are doing the same thing, they must know
something we don't. Especially when we are uncertain,
we are willing to place an enormous amount of trust in the
collective knowledge of the crowd.

7. **Liking: The Friendly Thief**

AS A RULE, we prefer to say yes to the requests of
someone we know and like. The true request to purchase

the product does not come from a stranger, it comes from a friend. Take, for instance, the growing number of charity organizations that recruit volunteers to canvass for donations close to their own homes. They understand perfectly how much more difficult it is for us to turn down a charity request when it comes from a friend or a neighbor.

The company which specializes in door-to-door sales of various home-related products, advises its salespeople to use the "endless chain" method for finding new customers. Once a customer admits to liking a product, he or she can be pressed for the names of friends who would also appreciate learning about it. The individuals on that list can then be approached for sales and a list of their friends, who can serve as sources for still other potential customers, and so on in an endless chain.

The key to the success of this method is that each new prospect is visited by a salesperson armed with the name of a friend "who suggested I call on you. Turning the salesperson away, under those circumstances, is difficult; it's almost like rejecting the friend.

Most of us would have guessed that people are more willing to do a favour for someone they like. We prefer to purchase from the person who respects us or whom we like.

Why did customers like any salesman more than some other salesperson who offered a fair price?

1.Good-looking people have an advantage in social interaction.

2.A halo effect occurs when one positive characteristic of a person dominates the way that person is viewed by others.

3.One who sends each month to the former customer a holiday greeting card containing a personal message each. (Happy New Year or Happy Thanksgiving, etc.) The message printed on the face of the card never varied. It read, "I LIKE YOU." There is nothing else on the card.

"I like you." It came in the mail every year, twelve times a year, like clockwork. "I like you." On a printed card that went off to known customers.

Similarity

We like people who are similar to us. This fact seems to hold true whether the similarity is in the area of opinions. Several studies have demonstrated that we are more likely to help those who dress like us.

The sales records of insurance companies found that customers were more likely to buy insurance when the salesperson was like them in such areas as age, religion, politics, and habits. Because even small similarities can be effective in producing a positive response to another.

Many sales training programs now urge trainees to "mirror and match" the customer's body posture, mood, and verbal style, as similarities along each of these dimensions have been shown to lead to positive results.

There is a natural human tendency to dislike a person who brings us unpleasant information, even when that person did not cause the bad news.

8. **Authority:** Follow an expert

A multi-layered and widely accepted system of authority confers an immense advantage upon a society. This property of authority status may account for much of its success as a compliance device. Not only does it work forcefully on us, but it also does so unexpectedly.

Thus, physicians, who possess large amounts of knowledge and influence in this vital area, hold the position of respected authorities. No one may overrule the doctor's judgment in a case, except perhaps, another doctor of higher rank.

Titles: Titles are simultaneously the most difficult and the easiest symbols of authority to acquire. To earning one normally takes years of work and achievement.

Clothes: The second kind of authority symbol that can trigger our mechanical compliance is clothing. Once, I entered a hospital during a slot of restricted time, without any permission, and no one raised any objection to refusing my entry because I was dressed so nicely that I looked like a doctor. Everything about clothing sends a message of propriety and respectability.

Trappings: Aside from their function in uniforms, clothing can symbolize a more generalized type of authority when it serves an ornamental purpose. Fincly styled and expensive clothes carry an aura of status and position, as do trappings such as jewellery and cars.

9. Scarcity: The Rule of the Few

"The way to love anything is to realise that it might be lost." G.K. Chesterton

Since that encounter with the scarcity principle—opportunities seem more valuable to us when their availability is limited. When the customer is informed that a certain product is in short supply that cannot be guaranteed to last long. Sometimes the limited number of information was true, sometimes it was wholly false. But in each instance, the intent was to convince customers of an items scarcity and thereby increase its immediate value in their eyes.

In accordance with the scarcity principle, the customers are asked to commit to buying the appliance when it looks least available—and therefore most desirable. Many customers do agree to purchase at this singularly vulnerable time.

Related to the limited number technique is the "deadline" tactic, in which some official time limit is placed on the customers opportunity to get what the compliance professional is offering.

The Scarcity Principle was employed during the second and third phone calls, "buy quickly without thinking too much about it." Click the link.

Customers are often told that unless they make an immediate decision to buy, they will have to purchase the item at a higher price, or they will be unable to purchase it at all.

The scarcity principle is more effective at some times than at other times. During Covid-19 the value of Oxygen cylinders was increased due to a shortage of supply against demand. Once again, we see that a less-available item is more desired and valued.

Psychological Reactance

According to the theory, whenever a free choice is limited or threatened, the need to retain our freedoms makes us desire them significantly more than previously.

The principle involved has notable power in directing human action. In this case, because we know that the things that are difficult to possess are typically better than those that are easy to possess, we can often use an item's availability to help us quickly and correctly decide on its quality.

Tips to be a successful Salesman

***Active Listener**: They properly listen to the requirements of their customers and take

   intcrest in their conversation.

***Play the Game of Name Card:** They call their customers by their names with respect.

   Calling by name creates friendships with customers.

***Creates Trust:** By sharing the secrets of the product, they try to create Trust with the customers. This can also be possible to give an extra discount to show that they are a special customer to him.

***Roots of Interest:** Find out the interest of the customer and try to share your experiences in the same field. When the customer cames to know that you also have the same interest, he will be bound to purchase from you.

***Magnetic Personality:** Create your friendship in such a way that the customers feel respected and happy to meet you. Each and everyone is interested to listen to the good thing about one's nature and try to praise for his interest by purchasing the product from him.

***Learn to say No**: If you do not like anything, try to say no with a respect.

"Until you cross the bridge of your insecurities,
You can't begin to explore possibilities."

Chapter-Five
How to Increase Your Wealth and Worth

Most of your competitors offer the same service and products. So the question is

"Why should people buy you?"

"Let your attitude attract someone because beauty is not a lifetime asset

People be so jealous of you because your character carries more weight than their title."

Two doctors have the same degree and the same experience.

One earns Rs.50000/- per month and the other earns Rs.5 lakh per month

Two advocates have the same education and the same experience.

One earns Rs.50000/- per month and the other earning Rs.5 lakh per month

Two Chartered Accountants have the same degree and the same experience.

One earns Rs.1 lakh per month and the other earns Rs.5 lakh per month

This is all due to their value and their worth in the eyes of others.

Why the peoples are ready to pay more?

How you can increase your value to earn more.

1.Develop Your Skill

Having the required education qualification is only a certificate that you are a qualified doctor. But to increase your knowledge you have to upgrade your skill and have to improve your knowledge as per the newly developed technologies. There is so much development in medical science and one has to learn the day-to-day developments. Those doctors who are doing their practice according to their old knowledge are earning less compared to the doctors who are doing their practice as per the latest technology & knowledge. Professionals who want to increase their income, have to develop their knowledge and skill.

2. Change your workplace

A bottle of two-litter Coca-Cola is sold for Rs.120 at the shop. The same coca-cola is sold for Rs.200 at the hotel but when we purchased the same bottle at the airport it will cost us Rs.300. If you want to increase your worth, you have to change your place of work where people acknowledge your value. A doctor will get the lowest fee if he is doing his practice in the village but at the same time, if he does his practice in a city, he will get more. A person should shift to the place where his worth increases.

3. Principle of Contrast: (a higher price typically reflects higher quality.)

There is a principle in human perception, the contrast principle, that affects the way we see the difference between two things. Consultancy Fees alone had become a trigger feather for quality, and a dramatic increase in the value of professionals.

4. Social Proof

The principle of social proof says so. The greater the number of people who find any idea correct, the more the idea will be correct. As a rule, Usually, when a lot of people are recommending someone, it is the right thing to do. And the person who is in demand can charge more fee because the crowd of people's recommendations has already increased his value

5. Authority: Follow an expert

A widely accepted system of authority confers an immense advantage upon a society. Thus physicians who possess large amounts of knowledge and influence in any vital area, hold the position of respected authorities. The Authority of a professional person in his field of work attracts more fees and value. A title like is simultaneously the most difficult and the easiest symbol of authority to acquire. Earning one normally takes years of work and achievement.

6. Scarcity: The Rule of the Few

Since that encounter with the scarcity principle— opportunities seem more valuable to us when their availability is limited. There is always a shortage of experienced and skilled & knowledgeable people, and their scarcity increases their value.

7. Law of Demand and supply

A product that is easily available has lower value whereas people are ready to pay more for a product having a shortage of supply.

8. Responsibility: A Manager who took full responsibility to handle all the operations in any unit is always getting a higher payout.

9.Working Conditions: The value of a person depends upon the working condition of a particular job. A person working in mines always gets a higher payout

"The sooner you start believing in yourself,
The sooner you'll start seeing results."

RECAP

Earning is not much difficult as compared to maintaining the earned wealth.

How you can have a check on your money spending

Tips for Money Management

1. Keep track of your spending.
2. Separate wants from needs
3. Avoid using credit to pay your bills
4. Save regularly.
5. Cut or downgrade your services
6. Try lowering your energy bill.
7. Cut down on take-out ordering.

GOLDEN RULE TO SUCCESS

1.Pay Yourself First

2.Save at least 20% of your Income

3.Have an Emergency Fund

4.Put your Money to Work

You should create these earned assets in your lifetime to earn income

1.Business

2.Real Estate / Land

3.Stock (Paper assets)

4.Gold & Silver

5.Cash in Hand

6.Equipmemt & Accessories

7.Copy right, Trademark, and Patents

8.Brand name

9.Network

10.Website

You can have as much cash with you in your home or in your business provided:

1. You can prove the source of cash with you.

2. You have proof to show why you are having that much cash with you and it is properly accounted for if it is related to business.

3. If you do not have valid proof for holding cash over its limits, then you may have to pay a 137% of penalty on the total unaccounted cash with you.

4. Any *person can carry Rs.*250000 without any type of documents, if a *person carries* more than Rs.2.5 Lakhs then he/she must *carry* any proof or have to prove the source.

5. There is a limit of Rs. 25,000 per person for Indian residents to carry from India to the US.

The circular issued by CBDT specifies that a married lady is allowed to keep up to 500 grams of gold jewelry; an unmarried lady can hold up to 250 grams and a male member of the family can keep up to 100 grams of gold ornaments and jewellery.

Tips to be a successful Salesman

***Active Listener**: They properly listen to the requirements of their customers and take interest in their conversation.

***Play the Game of Name Card:** They call their customers by their names with respect. Calling by name creates friendships with customers.

***Creates Trust:** By sharing the secrets of the product, they try to create Trust with the customers. This can also be possible to give an extra discount to show that they are a special customer to him.

***Roots of Interest:** Find out the interest of the customer and try to share your experiences in the same field. When the customer came to know that you also have the same interest, he will be bound to purchase from you.

***Magnetic Personality:** Create your friendship in such a way that the customers feel respected and happy to meet you. Each and everyone is interested to listen to the good thing about one's nature and try to praise for his interest by purchasing the product from him.

***Learn to say No**: If you do not like anything, try to say no with a respect.

How you can increase your value to earn more

1.   Develop your skill

2.   Change your workplace

3.   Principle of contract

4.   Social Proof

5.   Authority

6.   Scarcity

7. Law of Demand & Supply
8. Responsibility
9. Working conditions

Stage-6
Look, Listen & Learn

Chapter-One
Financial Knowledge

"The mind is the limit. As long as the mind can envision the fact that you can do something, you can do it –as long as you really believe 100 percent. (Arnold Schwarzenegger)

ESSENTIALS TO SUCCESS

 Your biggest strength is your mindset. You are the master of your fate because you have the power to control your thoughts. When a man really DESIRES a thing so deeply that he is willing to stake his entire future on a single turn of the wheel in order to get it, he is sure to win. We must magnetize our minds with intense Desire for the rich, and we must become "money conscious until the DESIRE for money drives us to create definite plans for acquiring it.

1.Visualize your Success

2.Meditate on a Daily Basis

3.Always think Bigger

4.Create a Life Plan

5.Be Grateful

Mindset of Rich People and Common mindset people

1. Rich-minded people invest in themselves. But a middle-class man thinks it's a wastage

2. Rich people learn to earn high-income skills

3. Rich people purchase first the Asset and then make Expenses

4. Rich people learn how to take Leverage

   * OPT (other people's time)

   * OPM (other people's money)

5. Rich people take massive action while common people only think

Seven Things That Rich People Teach Their Kids That Poor Don't

1.Surround yourself with Successful People

2.Success is not Free

3.Have an abundance mentality.

4.Solve problems and get Rich

5.Keep making Assets

6.Replicate your Income

7.Money solve money problem

If you are one of those who believe that hard work and honesty, alone, will bring riches. It is not true.

The most intelligent man living may not succeed in accumulating money without plans which are practical and workable.

As Dr. Joseph Murphy explained in his famous book" The Power of your Subconscious Mind."

The feeling of wealth produces wealth; keep this in mind at all times. Your subconscious mind is like a bank, a sort of universal financial institution. It magnifies whatever you deposit or impress upon it whether it is the idea of wealth or of poverty.

Every morning as you awaken deposit thoughts of prosperity, success, wealth, and peace.

Your subconscious mind controls all the vital processes and functions of your body and knows the answer to all problems.

Remember that the real riches are in your mind. Don't make money your sole aim. Claim wealth, happiness, peace, true expression, and love, and personally radiate love and goodwill to all. Then your subconscious mind will give you compound interest in all these fields of expression.

"You can't cross the sea merely by standing and staring at the water."

Chapter-Two
Experience and Knowledge Make You Rich:

One of my favourite quotes is by American entrepreneur- Jim Rohn: "Formal education will make you a living; self-education will make you a fortune."

Formal education is increasingly vocational training to climb the corporate ladder.

I have found that self-education is the single most important activity in which I have invested most of my time and money. Learning by doing and self-education is the creative path to more meaningful work a deeply fulfilling life.

By the time computer was introduced and a new age of the computer started. I did not want to be left behind. The branded computer was costly I hired a hardware engineer to assemble a computer for me. I learned a few basics from my children and the required programs had to learn by myself from books like Tally (Accounting), Excel, and word. I wanted to be perfect in computer accounting and wanted to learn new software and programs. I started working from my home doing Computer Accounting and Tax consultancy and I was surprised that my monthly earnings increased as compared to my salary earned. This was all due to my experience in so many companies and doing different types of work which enhanced my skill.

Earning money is no problem for me. I want to learn Network Marketing the new business concept. Became a Life and Health Insurance advisor. And it made me financially secure because doing any one policy gave a commission for more than 10 years just like a pension and there was no limit to earning. If you are willing to work, if you are willing to learn and if you have a burning desire to become successful then money will be your employee and will work for you 24/7 without paying any salary. I like this quote:

My interest is in the future because I am going to spend the rest of my life there. (Charles F. Kettering)

RULES OF MONEY: LEARN HOW TO EARN MONEY PASSIVELY

Chapter Three
Achieving Financial Success

"I will prepare and someday my chance will come."
(Abraham Lincoln)

Each of us has many, many plans in our head and we simply assume that the way we see things is the way they really are or the way they should be. Our character basically is a composite of our habits. Habits are powerful factors in our lives.

8 HABITS OF FINANCIALLY SUCCESSFUL PEOPLE

1) **They make a Plan**: Making a budget, sticking to it and framing goals are the essential components of formulating a plan.

2) **They don't Put off Decisions**: Delay can not only result in monetary losses but also lead to avoidable confusion and legal hassles.

3) **They are Proactive**: Make sure that they research before making an investment choice and keep track of regulatory changes to avoid losses and scams.

4) **They don't React Impulsively**: Wait before taking action and avoid 'attractive' options.

5) **They Review their Portfolio**: Monitoring is critical to know if they are on course.

6) **They Diversify their Investments**: Follow this golden rule of investment to avoid the risk of concentration.

7) **They Avoid Bad Debts**: To plug a hole in their savings, beware of these loans.

8) **The Cover Risks**: By securing insurance, they make sure that their dependents and investments are protected.

A few habits of the highly effective people as explained in the book **"The7 Habits of Highly effective people"**

a) **Be Proactive**: We can evaluate and learn from others' experiences as well as our own. Self-awareness enables us to stand apart and examine even the way we "see" ourselves. The only vision we have of ourselves comes from the social mirror of the people around us. It means that as human beings, we are responsible for our own lives. Our behavior is a function of our decisions. We have the initiative and the responsibility to make things happen. **They do not blame circumstances.**

'I am what I am today because of the choices I made yesterday." That person cannot say, "I choose otherwise." Proactive people focus their efforts on the work and on the things they can do something about with positive energy.

b). **Begin with the End in Mind:** To start with a clear understanding of your destination. It means to know where you are going so that you better understand where you are now and so that the steps you take are always in the right direction. **The carpenter's rule is "measure twice, cut once,"** You have to make sure that the blueprint, the first creation, is really what you want, and that you have thought everything through. **Most business failures begin in the first creation, with problems such as under-capitalization, misunderstanding of the market, or lack of a business plan.**

c). **Put First Things First**: To say "yes" to important priorities, you have to learn to say no" to other activities, sometimes apparently urgent things. Your tool should help you to keep balance in your life to identify your various roles and keep them right in front of you so that you do not neglect important areas such as your health, your family, professional preparation, or personal development.

Your planning tool should be your servant, never your master, since it has to work for you, it should be tailored to your style, your needs, and your particular ways. Your tool should also be portable so that you can carry it with you most of the time. If your organizer is portable, you will keep it with you **so that important data is always within reach.**

d). **Think Win / Win:** A person with the Win mentality thinks in terms of securing his own ends—and leaving it to others to secure theirs. **And if I focus on my own Win and do not even consider others' points of view, there is no basis for any kind of productive relationship**. Public Victory does not mean victory over other people. It means success in effective interaction that brings mutually beneficial results to everyone involved.

e). Seek First to Understand. Then to be Understood: Unless I open up with you **unless you understand me and my unique situation and feeling, you won't know how to advise or counsel me**. The professional learn how to diagnose, and how to understand. He also learns how to relate people's needs to his products and services. If you are dealing with people you are close to, it's helpful to tell them what you are doing. You can always seek first to understand. You have accurate information to work with, you get to the heart of matters quickly, you build Emotional, and give people the psychological air they need so you can work together effectively.

f). Synergize: You can sidestep negative energy, **you can look for the good in others and utilize that good**, as different as it may be, to improve your point of view and enlarge your perspective. **Think about a person who typically sees things differently than you do.** Consider ways in which those **differences might be used as stepping-stones** to a third alternative solution. Identify a situation in which you desire greater teamwork.

g). Sharpen the Saw: Make a list of activities that would help you keep in good physical shape, that would fit your lifestyle, and that you could enjoy over time. Select one of the activities and list it as a goal in your personal role area for the coming week. At the end of the week evaluate your performance.

Nine Habits of Wealthy People
1. They wake up early.
2. They meditate.
3. They don't watch TV, they read
4. They write a to-do list the night before.
5. They keep themselves busy.
6. They network.
7. They know when to say No.
8. They manage their money
9. They set Goals and Visualize

"Opportunity doesn't make appointments,
You have to be ready when it arrives."

Chapter Four
Business Lessons from the Top Businessmen

"You can study, watch videos, or read books all you want, but nothing is going to replace action."

Money Lessons We Can Learn from Mukesh Ambani

When the wealthiest man in the country, who is a thriving conglomerate and one of the finest business minds, continues to match the path of unabated success, then success is not measured in money alone. With his charter of success, he turns into an inspiration to millions of minds who would want to borrow the genie (guardian spirit that is assigned to each person at birth) from him.

When a businessman speaks of his success and what kept him going, he does so from his experience and would generalize it to suit a large section of the listeners who are hoping to follow in his footsteps to achieve success and money. The better you understand your business ecology, your efforts are sure to meet successful. Below are 8 money lessons we learned from Mukesh Ambani:

1.Money is a by-product

Mukesh Ambani's father 'Dhirubhai' said money is a by-product and chasing money alone would never make anybody a successful businessman.

2. Have a Dream

Like money is not a means to an end, money is not a dirty word in Reliance. Mukesh believes having a dream and working towards it is the most essential thing for any business to identify its niche space. Words may sound hollow when one speaks of a 'dream' but, really how can a business take shape without a concept and a dream that would show the road ahead?

3. Revenue figures speak louder

Mukesh Ambani's Reliance is almost everywhere, but the man barely has the time to be 'seen' in the media. When work speaks, everything else falls silent. .And when the company is on a growth trajectory, you needn't worry about being 'seen'. After all, revenue figures do matter more than anything else.

4. Trust all but depend on none.

When it comes to work, Mukesh Ambani knows nothing can match the aspects of perseverance and self-learning. There is no bitterness here but having waded through some difficult situations himself at a very young age, Mukesh has been a very hands-on - leader who knows the last nuance of his work. Trust is something but being prepared for all kinds of emergencies is what keeps the company going- he knows it well.

5. Risks give the greatest lessons

There is a fundamental difference between an adventure-seeker and a gambler. Both set out to make memorable experiences. But both choose different ways to do so. Mukesh is more of an adventure seeker than a gambler. He knows his goals and will chase them to their logical end.

6.Build team-morale

Be there for your team. Trust the professionals. Learn, learn, and learn. It's never too late for that. When you build teams that are trustworthy, every moment you spend with them contributes directly to the revenue of the company.

7. Stay alert, on-guard

It always pays well to understand your surroundings. You may have created a niche product. But if there is a better product in the market that's going to outdo, you better pull up your socks and sit down to improve your skills. A product is not sacrosanct. Competition always yields a better deal to the customer.

8. Credibility carries a high premium

Whether your team needs you, and your competition, be there on both occasions to give your fullest. Understand, innovate, and prepare for the future. If you settle into your resting chair, and you will be the biggest loser. Credibility is something that needs to be safeguarded beyond your cash inflow and outflow.

BUSINESS LESSONS FROM THE TOP VISIONARIES
(From the book "Top Visionaries who changed the world)

Your start in life is not what is most important, it is where you end up that counts.

STEVE JOBS: (Most powerful person in business and the greatest innovator of Apple)

Jobs would say that you should not just aim to be an entrepreneur or an investor. You must be a revolutionary too. **Don't sell products, sell dreams**.

1. **Work with the best people in the business**. If you want to develop the best products in the world, you need the best people in every post. **Trust the people you appoint** and invest time, money, and effort into your commercial relationships.

2. **Always be a step ahead of the competition**. You need to look into the future and anticipate customer needs and wants. Staying ahead requires you to have a never-ending stream of new ideas.

3. **Believe passionately in what you do**. To be a success, you will have to commit all your time, energy, and money to your project

4. **Getting something wrong doesn't mean you have failed**. Jobs launched some dud products. He got kicked out of his own company. He didn't let it get him down. He got back up and fought on. He looked critically at himself and realized what he had done wrong and learned important lessons for the future. We all have to change, and we all have room to improve.

5. **Be the change you want to see in the world**. He branched out beyond computing, encouraging other sectors to prioritize innovation and quality too. And then breaking his own records continue at Apple and in Silicon Valley as a whole, long after jobs' death.

JACK MA (Instigator of China's rise to the first position in the market of most successful e-commerce firm in the world, the Alibaba Group)

1. **He believes that attitude is far more important than capabilities**.

2. **Leaders never compare their technical skills with employees** because an employee should always have superior technical skills. If not, then they hired the wrong person.

3. **A leader's job is to lead**—employees are the ones who actually perform the tasks.

4. **Giving up is the biggest failure in life**. Only by facing hardships can one become resilient enough to achieve success.

BILL GATES (The Richest Man in the World. His name has become synonymous with innovation and leadership in the software industry.)

His business acumen primely rests on the following principles

1. **There is a range of qualities in him**, openness to risk, focus, to the ability to think laterally were all instrumental in his success.

2. **His appetite for both risk and competition**, his brilliant intellect and inclination towards lateral thinking, and his

impressive dedication and focus all help fuel much of his business success.

3.**His adaptability to change**, handling of adversity, and ability to be humble despite his enormous success.

4.**His remarkable foresight** to fill a gap in the market before the market even existed.

5. **His object was to put laptops in every classroom in America**.

6.**Gates also helped to drive the change** that has altered in a very fundamental way, how we all live our lives. The enormous success of Microsoft helped the industry expand in terms of investment, innovation, and accessibility.

MARK ZUCKERBERG (Generated billion dollars with the creation of a single product: Facebook)

It is never too soon to discover your passion and start developing your ideas.

You need to be excited about what you create. If an idea doesn't thrill you, it won't thrill anyone else either.

1.**If you have an idea, develop it**. And if it doesn't work out, have another idea, and develop that one too. Eventually, you will come up with an idea that you are satisfied with and which is commercially viable.

2. **When you have found that idea, focus on it**. Zuckerberg has focused on Facebook every single day for over a decade.

3. If you can **tap into our desire** and need to engage with one another, in a way that is effective, you have the basis for a successful company.

4.**Give back to the society you live and work in**. You have a responsibility to contribute your time, money, energy, and ideas to make the world you live in, a better place.

5.**Don't overlook your personal life** if you want to be truly rich.

6.**Your ultimate goal is not just to make money**, but to have fulfilling life and to play a positive role in the world.

WARREN BUFFETT (World's greatest investor and second richest man)

"No matter how great the talent or efforts, some things just take time. You can't produce a baby in one month by getting nine women pregnant."

"The best education you can get is investing in yourself. But this doesn't always mean college or university."

"You only have to do very few things right in your life so long as you do not do too many things wrong."

"It takes 20 years to build a reputation and five minutes to ruin it. If you think about that, you will do things differently."

"The most important thing to do if you find yourself in a hole is to stop digging."

Never give up searching for the job that you are passionate about. Try to find the job you'd have if you were independently rich, Forget about the pay. When you are associating with the people that you love doing what you love, it doesn't get any better than that.

ARNOLD SCHWARZENEGGER (World-famous bodybuilder "Mr. Universe", Hollywood movie star, and Governor of California)

Progress in life depends on action. Learn from others, think about how to apply those lessons in your own life

The resistance that you fight physically in the gym and the resistance that you fight in life can only **build a strong character**.

Set your ambitions sky-high and don't settle for the second best.

Sometimes opportunities arise when you are not expecting them.

The mind is the limit. As long as the mind can envision the fact that you can do something, you can do it as long as you really believe 100%

1. **No business is too simple, or too humble**. There is money to be made everywhere.

2. **Take advice from people you admire and learn from them.**

3. **People do not become successful by accident**. Making your goals a reality requires sustained effort, often over many years. He has never lost sight of the fact that even when opportunities do come his way, he must still be the driving force behind his career if he wants to succeed.

4. **Decide what you are going to do and give it your all.**
   There is no point in making a half-hearted attempt at
   something. If you focus your attention and effort and put
   in the hours, you will achieve far more. Give what you do
   100%, and you then stand a far greater chance of making
   it to.

5. **Be open to opportunities and capitalize on them**. It
   happens throughout your life, doors open to you, and they
   are not always the ones you are expecting. You have to
   keep your mind open to new ideas and possibilities and
   make use of your existing platforms, skills, contacts, and
   experiences to pursue them.

RULES OF MONEY: HAVE A PLAN AND SET GOALS

"Words can inspire, thoughts can provoke, but only action
truly brings you closer to your dreams."

Chapter Five
Sins That Are Costing You Money

"You can't reach for anything new if your hands are still full of yesterday's junk."

1) LUST:- "I want..." could be the most dangerous words for your finances. Separate your expenses into discretionary, necessary, and luxury.

2) WRATH:- "I picked a good stock, but ran into bad luck." "I work so hard in the office, but the boss is partial and does not give me a raise".

Invest in your career by re-skilling, and working with a high performer to learn how to do the job right.

3) PRIDE:-It is always difficult to admit you are wrong. So, if a stock you considered a great pick has tanked, swallow your pride and admit that you made a wrong decision. Set a stop-loss order for all your stock. If the share price falls below a certain limit, sell it.

4) ENVY:-Envy could lead you into the big black hole of debt, and escaping it can be rather difficult. It may be tough, but living within your means is the only way to financial independence. A loan is good only if it helps you build an asset that will grow in value, otherwise, avoid taking one.

5) SLOTH:- Pay your bills in time to avoid penalties. And make a financial calendar. Check it every month to ensure that you don't miss out on any goal. Plan well in advance for your goals and re-balance your asset allocation regularly to achieve them.

6) GREED:- "Buy one, get two free.", "Low-interest rate of only 7%" So, if you are a conservative investor and can't take the heat, avoid day trading and speculation, and don't be obsessed with high returns. Fix a specific target for your investments, and when you achieve it, redeem the investment.

"Work with what you have: don't focus on what you don't have. Focus on your abilities and not your perceived limitations."

RECAP

Your biggest strength is your mindset. You are the master of your fate because you have the power to control your thoughts. When a man really DESIRES a thing so deeply that he is willing to stake his entire future on a single turn of the wheel in order to get it, he is sure to win. We must magnetize our minds with intense Desire for the rich, and we must become "money conscious until the DESIRE for money drives us to create definite plans for acquiring it.

1. Visualize your Success

2. Meditate on a Daily Basis

3. Always think Bigger

4. Create a Life Plan

5. Be Grateful

I have found that self-education is the single most important activity in which I have invested most of my time and money. Learning by doing and self-education is the creative path to more meaningful work and a deeply fulfilling life.

Each of us has many plans in our head and we simply assume that the way we see things is the way they really are or the way they should be. Our character, basically is a composite of our habits. Habits are powerful factors in our lives.

Nine Habits of Wealthy People

    1. They wake up early.

    2. They meditate.

    3. They don't watch TV, they read

    4. They write a to-do list the night before.

    5. They keep themselves busy.

    6. They network.

    7. They know when to say No.

    8. They manage their money

    9. They set Goals and Visualize

your business ecology, your efforts are sure to meet successful.

"The most important thing to do if you find yourself in a hole is to stop digging."

Never give up searching for the job that you are passionate about. Try to find the job you'd have if you were independently rich, Forget about the pay. When you are associating with the people that you love doing what you love, it doesn't get any better than that.

Stage-7
Health is Wealth

Don't forget to enjoy life while chasing your dreams.

There's nothing more important than our good health, that's our Principal Capital Asset.

When you have good health, you love everything in life. Because if you are fit and healthy you can earn and buy whatever you want. But being financially wealthy does not assure you your health and no amount of money can buy back health once it is lost. So always focus on your health first and don't lose your health in the run for the money.

Most Adult Problems can be avoided if you

1. Live below your means
2. Eat real food
3. Do what you love for work
4. Get a second income source
5. Work out at least 3 times per week
6. Get 3 True Friends

HOW TO ENJOY A HEALTHY LIFE

"It is Health that is Real Wealth and not pieces of Gold and Silver."—Mahatma Gandhi

The Greatest Wealth is Health. "Good Health is True Wealth."—Urijah Faber

The first wealth is health. Good health is the foundation on which to build a happy life.

You can't enjoy wealth if you are not in good health.

The first and most important thing is health care. Freedom of finance can be enjoyed only by a healthy person otherwise what is the use of earning more and more.

Healthcare expenses are a big component of overall retirement expenses. Hence, it is important to take health insurance at an early stage in one's life.

FOCUS........

I was jogging one day, and I noticed a person in front of me, about 1/4 of a mile. I could tell he was running a little slower than me and I thought, good, I shall try to catch him. I had about a mile to go my path before I needed to turn it off.

So I started running faster and faster. I was determined to catch him.

Finally, I did it! I caught and passed him by. On the inside, I felt so good.

"I beat him" of course, he didn't even know we were racing.

After I passed him, I realized I had been so focused on competing against him that I had missed my turn. I had gone nearly six blocks past it. I had to turn around and go all back. Isn't that what happens in life when we focus on competing with co-workers, neighbors, friends, and family, trying to outdo them, or trying to prove that we are more successful or more important?

We spend our time and energy running after them and we miss out on our own paths to our God-given destinies.

The problem with unhealthy competition is that it's a never-ending cycle.

There will always be somebody ahead of you, someone with a better job, a nicer car, more money in the bank, more education, a prettier wife, a more handsome husband, better- behaved children, etc. But realize that "You can be the best that you can be, you are not competing with anyone." Some people are insecure because they pay too much attention to what others are doing, where others are going, wearing, or driving.

Take what God has given you, the height, weight personality. Dress well, and wear it proudly! You'll be blessed by it.

Stay focused and live a healthy life.

There's no competition in DESTINY, run your own RACE and wish others WELL!!!

The secret of your future is hidden in your daily routine
1. Stay Active, don't retire
2. Take it Slow
3. Don't fill your Stomach
4. Daily gentle exercise
5. Connect with Nature
6. Live in the Moment
7. Surround yourself with good Friends
8. Follow your Passion
9. Smile
10. Be Grateful

Chapter One
The Japanese Secret to a Long and Happy Life—— IKIGAI

Our ikigai is hidden deep inside each of us, and finding it requires a patient search.

IKIGAI

PASSION	PROFESSION	VOCATION	MISSION
What you love	What you can be paid for	What you are good at	What the world needs

Ikigai map has four simple directions to fitness

1. Do what you love
2. Do what you are good at
3. Do what the world needs
4. Do what you can be rewarded for.

One surprising thing you notice, living in Japan, is how active people remain after they retire. In fact, many Japanese people never really retire— they keep doing what they love for as long as their health allows.

Not only do they live much longer than the rest of the world's population, but they also suffer from fewer chronic illnesses such as cancer and heart disease; inflammatory disorders are also less common.

Their blood tests reveal fewer free radicals (which are responsible for cellular aging), as a result of drinking tea and eating until their stomachs are only 80% full.

Members of these communities manage their time well in order to reduce stress, consume little meat or processed foods, and drink alcohol in moderation.

Their diet is rich as they eat sweet potatoes, fish (three times per week), and vegetables.

It has been shown that maintaining an active, adaptable mind is one of the key factors in staying young.

Ten Rules of ikigai

1. **Stay active; don't retire**

2. **Take it slow.** As the old saying goes. **"Walk Slowly and You Will Go Far."**

3. **Don't fill your stomach.** 80% rule. Eating until their stomachs are only 80% full

4. **Surround yourself with good friends.** Friends are the best medicine

5. **Get in shape for your next birthday.** The body you move through life needs a bit of daily maintenance to keep it running for a long time. Do exercise.

6. **Smile.** A cheerful attitude is not only relaxing—but it also helps make friends.

7. **Reconnect with nature.** We should return to it often to recharge our batteries

8. **Give thanks.** To everything that brightens your days and makes you feel lucky to be alive

9. **Live in the moment. Stop regretting the past and fearing the future.** Today is all you have. Make the most of it. Make it worth remembering.

10. **Follow your ikigai. There is a passion inside you, a unique talent that gives meaning to your days and drives you to share the best of yourself until the every end.**

What I learned?

For a Healthy and Happy Life (Follow three "S")

1. Go Slow (Don't be in Hurry)

2. Be Silent (listen more and Speak less)

3. Keep Smiling (Put a smile on Someone's Face)

1	+0	+0	+0	+0	10000
Health	Work	Money	Family	Dreams	

Without one everything else is zero.

"Health is like money. We never have a true idea of its value untile we lose it."

RECAP

HEALTH IS WEALTH

When you have good health, you love everything in life. Because if you are fit and healthy you can earn and buy whatever you want. But being financially wealthy does not assure you your health and no amount of money can buy back health once it is lost. So always focus on your health first and don't lose your health in the run for the money.

The first wealth is health. Good health is the foundation on which to build a happy life.

You can't enjoy wealth if you are not in good health.

The first and the most important thing is health care. Freedom of finance can be enjoyed only by a healthy person otherwise what is the use of earning more and more.

60 Financial Tips from "Mastering The Rich Mindset"

1. Don,t be a hater of money.

2. You need to be financially literate and know how to read financial statements. Profit & Loss, Balance Sheet (Asset & Liabilities)

3. Keep expenses low, Reduce liabilities.

4. Concentrate your efforts on buying income-producing Assets. First purchase Income generating Asset than comfort.

5. Never depend on a single income. Make investments to create a second source. One income should be to pay for your needs and wants. And the other income is for Investment.

6. It is mostly said: (INCOME – EXPENSES = SAVING), but actually, it should be: (INCOME – SAVING = EXPENSES)

7. If you have not saved during your twenties, then now you have to save 30% to 50% of your income for the future.

8. You should spend less on your kids besides the expenses of their educations.

9. If you have no house of your own. Now at the age of 40 years, it's not good to take a home loan for a long period of time.

10. Health is more important. You have to buy health insurance for at least 5 lacs.

11. And moreover, you have to take term insurance at least for one crore.

12. You must have an Emergency Fund with you. Buy at least 10 grams of Gold so that in any emergency you may sell it.

13. Reduce your Debts to Nil.

14. Don't purchase if it is not essential.

15. Make sure that your saving is sufficient to beat inflation.

16. Use the law of compounding for investment to beat inflation. Compound interest means you not only earn returns on the principal money that you invest but also get to enjoy a return on the interest income that keeps adding to your principal.

17. Invest in Stock Market or Mutual Fund. The safest way is to start a SIP of MF in the Index Fund of Nifty Fifty only. The rate of return might be 1% low for MF, but it will be safe as an investment.

18. Make your Monthly Personal Budget (80/20). Pay-yourself-first. First save at least 20% of total income, and then freely spend the remaining 80%

19. Understand the law of Taxes. We can save more out of our income. If we understand to save our Tax liabilities.

20. Live life according to the money you have.

21. Pay your bills in time to avoid penalties.

22. Avoid taking loans if EMI is more than 30% of your total income.

     Five Tips for getting housing loan (5/20/30/40/50)
     1. Loan should not be more than 5 times of your annual income.
     2. Loan should not be more than 20 years.
     3. EMI should not be more than 30% of your monthly income.
     4. Housing Loan should not be taken after the age of 40 years.
     5. Total EMI of all the loans should not be more than 50 % of your monthly income.

23. Plan for your Retirement.

24. Invest your savings for making money and puts it into financial instruments or products such as shares, bonds, property, and even term deposits. Your investments can make your good times better and help you in your bad times.

25. Do not save what is left after spending but spend what is left after saving.

26. Your success in business depends upon three principles:
     1. Product or service: What you Sell?
     2. People willing to pay for it.
     3. Sell What People Buy.

27. Nothing will change your life faster than building new skills. Learn them via business books, and videos but don't forget to physically practice your skills too.

28. Don't buy a car until you Invest in some Income Generating Assets.

29. Three types of investment can grow your wealth
    1. In Equity Shares or Mutual Funds. If dividend income is more than the interest rate.
    2. In Gold. Not in Jewellery. You wouldn't get the correct value at the time of sale. It is better to invest in Gold Bonds.
    3. In Real Estate. If the rental income you receive is more than 8% of the Return on investment.

30. Plan your financial investments in such a way that after retirement you live a respectable life and that you do not feel a shortage of funds due to retirement.

31. If you want to attract more money, start thinking about your finances, how you are going to make more money, and how you are going to save.

32. Time is Money. We should value time as much as we value money.

33. You can make your dreams come true if you have the right mindset, put in the right effort, and make a reasonable plan.

34. Earning is not much difficult as compared to maintaining the earned wealth. Check- on your money spending.

35. Outsource your work to Save your time.

36. Learn to Win. You should have a positive attitude and be optimistic. You should focus on "can" instead of "can't."

37. You shouldn't run away from difficult situations rather you face them and try to get out of them.

38. Restriction on Acceptance of Loans, Deposits, etc of Rs.20000 or more in Cash.

39. You can have as much cash with you in your home or in your business provided, you can prove the source of cash with you.

40. Any person can carry Rs.250000 without any type of documents, if a person carries more than Rs.2.5 Lakhs then he/she must carry any proof or have to prove the source.

41. Residents of India are allowed to carry up to Rs. 25,000. There's no limit, however, to how much foreign currency you can bring into India. Although, you will have to declare it if the amount exceeds US$ 5,000 in notes.

42. A married lady is allowed to keep up to 500 grams of gold jewellery; an unmarried lady can hold up to 250 grams and a male member of the family can keep up to 100 grams of gold ornaments and jewellery.

43. Rich-mndset people invest in themselves and learn to earn high-income skills.

44. Surround yourself with Successful People.

45. Every morning as you awaken deposit thoughts of prosperity, success, wealth, and peace. Your subconscious mind controls all the vital processes and functions of your body and knows the answer to all problems.

46. Formal education will make you a living, self-education will make you a fortune.

47. Make sure to research before making an investment choice and keep track of regulatory changes to avoid losses and scams.

48. To start with a clear understanding of your destination, so that you better understand where you are now and so that the steps you take are always in the right direction.

49. Habits of Successful People
* They make a plan.
* They don't Put off Decisions.
* They are Proactive.
* They Diversify their Investments.
* They Avoid Bad Debts.
* They know when to say No.
* They manage their money.
* They set Goals and Visualize.

50. Lessons from the Top Businessmen
* Have a Dream.
* Trust all but depend on none.
* Build team-morale.
* Credibility carries a high premium.
* Don't sell products, sell dreams.
* Work with the best people in the business.
* Always be a step ahead of the competition.
* Believe passionately in what you do.
* Getting something wrong doesn't mean you have failed.
* An employee should always have superior technical skills.
* When you have found an idea, focus on it.
* Progress in life depends on action.
* Set your ambitions sky-high and don't settle for the second best.

* Take advice from people you admire and learn from them.
* There is no point in making a half-hearted attempt at something.

51. "I want..." could be the most dangerous words for your
    finances. Separate your expenses into necessary, and luxury.

52. A loan is good only if it helps you build an asset that will grow
    in value, otherwise, avoid taking one.

53. "Buy one, get two free.", "Low-interest rate" , avoid day
    trading and speculation.

54. There's nothing more important than our good health, that's
    our Principal Capital Asset

55. Freedom of finance can be enjoyed only by a healthy person.

56. Healthcare expenses are a big component of overall retirement
    expenses. Hence, it is important to take health insurance at
    an early stage in one's life.

57. There's no competition in DESTINY, run your own RACE
    and wish others WELL.

58. The secret of your future is hidden in your daily routine.
    1. Stay Active, don't retire.
    2. Take it Slow.
    3. Surround yourself with good Friends.
    4. Follow your Passion.

59. Stop regretting the past and fearing the future. Today is all
    you have. Make it worth remembering.

60. There is a passion inside you, a unique talent that gives meaning
    to your days and drives you to share the best of yourself.

Conclusion : The rich mindset is a powerful tool for achieving financial success and living a wealthy lifestyle. By mastering the rich mindset, you can transform your life and achieve your financial goals. We hope this book has provided you with the tools and strategies you need to develop a rich mindset and live the life you've always dreamed of.

Last but not least,

keep it in your mind.

You don't learn how to swim by reading a book.

You need to jump in the water.

Motivation Business Quotes

1.How to begin the journey to be a millionaire

    a. Save more than you spend

    b. Build your knowledge of personal finance and investments

    c. Reach a debt-free status

    d. Think long-term investments

    e. Invest right from your first salary

    f. Invest your increments

    g. Get professional advice

2.Disappear for Six Months: * Don't go out to parties

    *Study all day long to learn high profitable skill (copywriting, web design, direct response marketing etc.)

    * Record your progress

    * Sell your skills online

    Those six months will change your life forever

3. **Lesson from Rich Dad Poor Dad**
    *crazy to listen
    *First invest on you
    *Invest on luxury later
    *Earn on your asset
    *Control your habits
    *Do not work for money
    *Be with intelligent persons
    *Life-long learning habits

4. **Don't think about saving money**,
    think about making more money.

5. **Most people**— have an idea— think about it—goes to sleep.
    The 1% has an idea—think about it——take action

6. **How to get rich as a marketer**.
    *Find a winning product
    *Develop a professional store / Funnel
    *Have a multistep marketing plan

7. **Focus on making $1 first**.
    Then focus on $10, Then $100,$1000, $10000 and so on. Don't get caught up in the long term when the short-term needs focus first.

8. **Successful people are not those who do not fail,**
    they are those who fail more than anyone &, simply refuse to accept it as the conclusion.

9. **Everything is easy,**

   when you are crazy for it.

   And nothing is easy when you are lazy for it.

10. **You don't get rich for Having Ideas**,

    you get Rich Making Them a Reality.

11. **The Rich don't work for Money.**

    They make Money work for them.

12. **If you are not doing What You Love**.

    You are Wasting Your Time

13. **Death is not the Greatest Loss in Life**.

    The Greatest Loss is what Dies Inside while still Alive.

    Never Surrender.

14. **Being Late doesn't mean failure**.

    Maybe it means getting ready for a Great Launch.

15. **Be Smart**

    * If you hang around 5 confident people, **you will be the 6th**

    * If you hang around 5 Intelligent people, **you will be the 6th**

    *If you hang around 5 millionaires, **you will be the 6th**

    * If you hang around 5 idiots, **you will be the 6th**

16. **THINK LONG-TERM**

    Plan for the next 6-12 months and take action every day

That is how you build a solid business

There is no secret, and you will not become Rich overnight

People who plan ahead get results

People who want success overnight never begin

17. Habits of Self- Made Millionaire:

1. Dream big dreams
2. Do what you love to do
3. See yourself as self-employed
4. Have a clear sense of direction
5. Refuse to consider the possibility of failure
6. Dedicate yourself in a lifelong learning.

18.SEVEN RULES TO WIN IN LIFE

*Have a Vision

*Growth is outside the comfort zone

*Don't compare yourself to others

* Make mistakes and learn from them

*Work smarter and harder than yesterday

*Expose yourself to new Ideas, Places and People

* Be Patient, but Persistent

19.SEVEN SIGNS YOU ARE GOING TO BE SUCCESSFUL IN YOUR LIFE

*You are continuously learning and applying.

*You don't let other people's opinions affect your mental peace and life

*You don't run away from difficult situations rather you face them and try to get out of them.

* You are kind and humble and always ready to help the needy

*You never settle and want to involve continuously.

*You know the value of time and don't let it go wasted

* You always gets up whenever you have setback in your life.

20.EIGHT THINGS TO MATTER

*Don't chase anyone

*Don't beg anyone to stay

*Know your worth

* Save space for people who matter

*Accept what cannot be changed

*Leave what is not for you

* Love yourself

*Take a step back and prioritise yourself

We get too busy with too many responsibilities in life that we forget how to take care of our own self.

21.EIGHT TIPS FOR BECOMING A MILLIONAIRE

*Steer Clear of Debt

*Invest Early

*Get Serious about your Saving

*Increase your Income to Reach Your Goal Faster

*Cut Unnecessary Expenses

*Keep Your Millionaire Goal Front and Centre

* Work with an Investing Professional

* Put Your Plan on Report

22. WHAT I WISH I KNEW WHEN I WAS 20:

*Save your income

* Educate yourself in investing

* Invest in assets

* Investing is a long-term game

* Live below your means

*Avoid instant gratification

* Material possessions don't matter

23. Easy to spot a yellow car when you are always thinking of a yellow car.

Easy to spot opportunity when you are always thinking of opportunityEasy to spot reasons to be mad when you are always thinking of being mad.

YOU BECOME WHAT YOU CONSTANTLY THINK ABOUT. Watch yourself

24. Passion+ Dream+ Purpose = CLARITY

Clarity+ Confidence+ Patience= SUCCESS

Story doesn't end here….

You become SUCCESSFUL + Now, INSPIRE others to do the same = MEANINGFUL LIFE

25. If hard work MADE YOU RICH,

Everyone with a 9-5 would be MILLIONAIRES

26. If you want to be SUCCESSFUL in life,

Then STOP taking advice from your friends, relatives etc. Follow & take advice only from those who live the same **QUALITY OF LIFE**

Which you DREAMT of for yourself

27. A WISE MAN SAID

"DON'T BE AFRAID TO START OVER AGAIN.

THIS TIME, YOU'RE NOT STARTING FROM SCRATCH,

YOU ARE STARTING FROM EXPERIENCE."

28. THE SECRET TO SUCCESS

HOW TO MAKE A RELATIONSHIP WITH YOUR DREAM & GOAL

WITHOUT RELATIONSHIP THERE IS NO POSSIBILITY TO SUCCEED IN LIFE

*Make it Visible or Obvious

It will repeatedly remind you about your dreams or goals

* Talk to your Dream

Power of visualization is real it will help you to build a connection with your dream

* Mix Emotions to your Dreams

Emotions provokes consistent actions

29. Financial Freedom

You wake up without an alarm

You are in no Rush

You plan out your day

You work on your own terms

You can take a break at any time

Read or exercise when you want to

30. **Thinking about doing something** Once you make money from investments, it's hard to spend because you view the cash as an opportunity to get more, not a voucher to waste.

31. **Someone graduated at 21, but waited 6 years to get a good job.**

Someone had no education, but was a millionaire by 21

You are not late

You are not early

You are on time

32. **It doesn't matter how slowly you go**

As long as you don't stop

33. **If you don't work to build your own dreams,**

then someone else will hire you for lifetime to build their dream.

34. **EVERY FAMILY has a person who breaks the chain of poverty**, Breaks the chain of profession, may you be the blessing to your entire family

35. **Twelve habits of successful people**

*Stand up straight with your shoulders back

*Treat yourself like someone you are responsible for helping

*Make friends with people who want the best for you.

*Compare yourself to who you were yesterday, not with someone else.

*Do not let your children do anything that makes you dislike them.

*Set your house in perfect order before you criticize the world

* live a meaningful life as to want to live

*Tell the truth or at least don't lie.

*Assume that the person you are listening to might know something you don't

*Be precise in your speech

*Do not bother children when they are skateboarding

*Pet a cat when you encounter one on the street

36. Being a little bit crazy is the key to success.

You can't do big things, thinking small

37. Too poor to start a business

The world's largest package delivery company
Was founded by two teenagers with a bicycle
And a $100 borrowed from a friend.
All you need is to have a problem-solving mindset.

38. You are capable of achieving anything you've

Ever dreamed of, you just have to want it badly enough

39. If you want to be successful in life, then stop taking advice

from your friends, relatives etc. Follow & take advice only
from those who live the same Quality of Life which you
Dreamt of for yourself.

40. **The biggest problem with most of the people is**:

They have no Clarity, about what they want?

Or

What, they don't want?

That's the only reason why most of the people live Middle-Class life.

41. **MENTAL TRICKS ONLY THE RICH USE**

- They tell themselves there's no shortage of money, even they don't have enough
- They think of making money as a game
- They block out fear
- They tell themselves that they deserve to be rich
- They set their expectations unreasonably high.

42. **YOU DON'T HAVE TO WORK TILL 65**

- 5-10 years of building income sources will make you financially free for life.
- Rental Property
- Dividend Stock
- E-commerce
- Side Hustles
- Online Business
- Social Media Marketing

Six / Month from each income source would generate $6K / Month

43. **ZEN OF LIFE**

What you feel you attract

What you imagine you create

What you think you become

44.**MIDDLE-CLASS have control over their Expenses only**, that's why they SAVE. RICH-CLASS have control over their INCOME also, that's why they INVEST

MIDDLE-CLASS always BUYS but, RICH-CLASS always SELLS.

If you want to be RICH, then LEARN TO SELL Otherwise, no one in this world ever become RICH by just BUYING & SAVING.

45.**BEST DECISIONS TO MAKE IN YOUR 20'S**
   * Waking up early
   * Creating multiple sources of income
   * Working out
   * Eating healthy
   * Reading Books
   * Investing in yourself
   * Learning a new skill
   * Travelling

46.**Appreciating your life despite not having what you want**, will give you the happiness that you strongly desire. Otherwise, you'll always go through life chasing things and suffering from the idea of not having them. Listen to your own voice, your own soul, too many people listen to the noise of the world, instead of themselves. Deep inside, you know what you want, let no one decide that for you.

47. BECOME A MILLIONAIRE

Do Action over Excuses

Books over Movies

Assets over Liabilities

Health over Money

Love over Hate

48. Success is a vehicle

* Which moves on a wheel

* Named hard work

* But the journey is Impossible

* Without the fuel named

* Self confidence

49. There are four types of wealth:

1* Financial wealth (money)

2* Social wealth (status)

3* Time wealth (freedom)

4* Physical wealth (health)

Be wary of jobs that lure you in with 1 and 2 but rob you of 3 and 4

50. BIGGEST MISTAKE EARLY ON IN CAREER WAS LIFESTYLE INFLATION

* Expensive CARS

* Expensive CLOTHES

* Expensive DINNERS

Once learned to live below means and invest money.

EVERYTHING CHANGED

Bibliography

1. Rich Dad Poor Dad, (Robert T. Kiyosaki)
2. Think and Grow Rich, (Napoleon Hill)
3. 7 Habits of Highly Effective People, (Stephen R. Covey)
4. The Power of Your Subconscious Mind, (Joseph Murphy)
5. The Warren Buffett Way, (Robert G. Hagstrom)
6. Who Stole the American Dream, (Burke Hedges)
7. IKIGAI, (Hector Gargia and Francesc Miralles)
8. Management Study Guide
9. "INFLUENCE" the book written, (Robert B. Cialdini)

www.ingramcontent.com/pod-product-compliance
Lightning Source LLC
Chambersburg PA
CBHW050725260726
48661CB00001B/64